A LIBRARY CLASSIFICATION
FOR CITY AND REGIONAL PLANNING

Harvard City Planning Studies, 18

Sponsored by the Graduate School
of Design, Harvard University

A LIBRARY CLASSIFICATION

FOR CITY AND REGIONAL PLANNING

Caroline Shillaber

A Revision of Pray and Kimball's
City Planning Classification of 1913

Harvard University Press
Cambridge, Massachusetts

1973

CONTENTS

Preface   vii

The Classification   1

Appendix A: Geographic Table   75

Index   83

PREFACE

    This little book is an updated edition of two
standard works on planning.

    City planning was first taught in this country in
1909 at Harvard University. Four years later, in 1913,
the first comprehensive classification of the literature
of city planning was prepared and published at Harvard.
The authors were James Sturgis Pray and Theodora Kimball.
Professor Pray was Chairman of the School of Landscape
Architecture, and Miss Kimball was that school's first
librarian. Frederick Law Olmsted, Jr., then teaching at
the school, made constructive suggestions. Both the wide
scope of the classification and its systematic arrangement
were reflected in the title, which was City Planning: A
Comprehensive Analysis of the Subject Arranged for the
Classification of Books, Plans, Photographs, Notes and
Other Collected Material with Alphabetic Subject Index.
It was published by Harvard University Press, which was
then only a few months old.

At that time there was no adequate provision for city planning in any library classification. The compilers decided to tie their work to the general classification scheme of the Library of Congress, in which Class N already stood for Fine Arts and the sub-class NA for Architecture. The Library of Congress formed a new sub-class, City Planning (NAC), to accommo date the Pray and Sturgis listings. (It also created a sub-class for Landscape Architecture and called it NAB.

The Pray and Sturgis book, analyzing NAC into numbered topics, is long since out of print; but, for sixty years, copies of it have been in continual use at Harvard and other institutions where city planning is being taught. The document has proved remarkably adapt able because of the wisdom of the compilers in foreseei the future. "Certain parts of the classification," the wrote, "must, of course, be expanded from time to time as the corresponding parts of the subject develop. The numbering of the scheme allows for this expansion." Accordingly, successive librarians at the Harvard Gradu School of Design (formed in 1935 by merging the School of Architecture, School of Landscape Architecture, and

School of City and Regional Planning) have added topics and sub-topics in longhand without altering the general structure of the original classification.

The present edition incorporates these piecemeal changes--and some brand-new ones--and provides librarians, planners, and students with a tool designed to meet the needs of the greatly expanded profession in the latter part of the twentieth century.

The new book includes also a similar revision of a classification published in 1937 covering broader fields of regional and national planning. This was <u>State and National Planning: An Analysis of the Subject Arranged with Particular Reference to the Classification of Library Material with Alphabetic Subject Index</u>, by Arthur C. Comey and Katherine McNamara in Collaboration with Henry V. Hubbard and Howard K. Menhinick and the U.S. National Resources Committee. The publisher again was Harvard University Press.

The two classifications as revised are here consolidated and printed in one sequence, and their subject indexes have been combined into one alphabetic list. This consolidated index is exceptionally full, and it includes, of course, all the additional topics that have been inserted in both classification schemes. The index refers the user to an NAC classification number rather than to a page. Where more than one number is given in the index or where there are cross references, the reason is usually that a subject can be considered from more than one point of view. This will present no problem in a large collection. In a collection that will remain small the person in charge may wish to concentrate material under one of the main subject headings rather than assigning it to a specific sub-topic.

Use of the classification in a small collection can be facilitated further by including subjects peripheral to planning. A study of economics _per se_, or statistics _per se_, can easily be assigned numbers within this scheme rather than in another Library of Congress system of classification.

In the present book, as in 1913, guidance for geographical classification is appended in a separate table (see page 77). This appendix is a reprinting of Table II from Library of Congress, _Classification: Class Fine Arts_, fourth edition, 1970. The original 1913 classification and the present revision provide for place names in two ways: (1) as major headings having specific numbers found in Table II, or (2) as sub-heads of any NAC number followed by g (for "geographical") and then by the Table II number.

Preparation of the present book has been generously encouraged and supported by Professor Lawrence D. Mann, Chairman of the Department of City and Regional Planning at Harvard. For careful typing I am grateful to Sharyn Kraus and especially to Mrs. Mary Yacubian whose meticulous typing has contributed to the accuracy of the work. Inevitably, in a revision, absolute accuracy is almost impossible where one change can generate many others. The compiler is also grateful for the cross-checking of the index by Eric Jahan.

Valuable suggestions and improvements have been contributed throughout the course of revision by Christopher Hail, Assistant Librarian.

Caroline Shillaber, Librarian
Harvard Graduate School of Design

February 1973

A LIBRARY CLASSIFICATION
FOR CITY AND REGIONAL PLANNING

NAC

If the Library of Congress classification
is used, precede numbers with NAC.

0   BIBLIOGRAPHY. General only. Special biblio-
    graphies go with the special subjects.

    PERIODICALS. Subdivided by language for general
    periodicals; local may file under 6800, City
    planning by countries and cities.

1   General

2   American and English

4   French

5   German

14 Other

14.5   Indexes and abstracts

15 Yearbooks

    SOCIETIES. Proceedings, sets of publications.
    For works on formation of societies, their
    activities, etc., see 513

20 General

21 International

22 United States

23 Latin America, South America, Central America,
    Mexico

25 Great Britain

25.1   Ireland

26 Canada

28 France and Belgium

29 Germany, Austria

31 Hungary, Czechoslovakia, Yugoslavia

32 Italy

33 Scandinavia, Netherlands

35 Spain and Portugal

36 Switzerland

39 Other

    CONGRESSES, CONFERENCES, CONVENTIONS

40 General

42 Permanent

46 Occasional

1

EXHIBITIONS
  Cf. 546, 940
50 General

52 International

55 United States

60 Europe

65 Other

MUSEUMS
70 General

    Local

75   United States

80   Europe

85   Other

90 LIBRARIES, PLANNING

91 Library science

92 Manuals

93 Classifications and subject headings

COLLECTED WORKS. General series
180 Several authors

185 Individual authors

190 ENCYCLOPAEDIAS, DICTIONARIES, GLOSSARIES,
     LISTS OF TERMS. WRITER'S MANUALS,
     PARLIAMENTARY PRACTICE, ETC.

195 DIRECTORIES

BIOGRAPHY
200 Collective

205 Individual, A-Z

HISTORY. Historical development of city plans,
    historic forms of city with examples. Cf.
    6800 - which is a geographical arrangement
210 Comprehensive, general

    European

212 General

    By Period

215	Ancient Cities
217	Preclassic
219	Classic
225	Mediaeval and Renaissance
227	Baroque
230	Modern
231	18th Century
232	19th Century
233	20th Century
235	East including Near East
240	North America
241	Pre-Columbian; Latin America
245	Africa, Pacific, Other

GENERAL WORKS

250	Comprehensive treatises
254	Outlines, syllabi, charts, diagrams, etc.
258	Pocket-books, tables, manuals, etc.
260	Partial works, treating two or more subdivisions of the general subject

Essays, addresses, lectures, poems

265	Collective. Miscellaneous
270	Single. City planning in literature. Fiction. When general; specific go with subject.
280	General collections of material in special forms. Classify here only material which is desired to be kept together as a collection rather than to be distributed by subject.
282	Atlases and maps and general collections of plans
284	Portfolios and general collections of paintings, illustrations, drawings, sketches, graphic arts, etc.
286	Albums and general collections of photographs, prints, plates, postcards, etc.
288	General collections of slides
290	General collections of clippings, excerpts, etc.
292	General collections of manuscripts, notes, etc.
294	General collections of books and pamphlets to be kept together as unique collections

295 Theses and dissertations

296 Reprints

300 Name. Use of terms and phrases. Quotations.
     City planning or Town planning, Civic design,
     Municipal improvement, Civic improvement,
     Civic betterment, Urban planning, Urban design,
     Community planning

305 Purpose, utility. Goals

310 Field, scope. Relation to other arts, sciences,
     and professions. Definition

     CITY PLANNING AS AN ART, SCIENCE OR PROFESSION
     Announcements and brochures, see 805

320 General

322 Requirements

324 Opportunities

     CITY PLANNING MOVEMENT. Municipal improvement,
     Civic betterment movement, etc.

500 General. Civic improvement

505 General special. Purposes, activities, pro-
     gress, etc.

     ORGANIZATION

510 General

     Agencies, organizations. Cf. 1525

512   General

513   Societies

515   Chambers of Commerce, Boards of Trade

517   Clubs, city clubs, women's clubs, juvenile
       leagues, etc.

518   Urban Coalition, ACTION groups, etc.

520 Resources

521 Foundations

525 Campaigns, organization of work, etc.

     EDUCATION OF PUBLIC. Awakening of interest,
     public advertising, publicity

540 General

542 Lectures. Cf. 265

543 Motion pictures, films, slides. Other audio-
     visual media

544   Publications, propaganda

546   Demonstrations, exhibitions, contests

547   Radio and study clubs

547.5 Television

548   Teaching in public schools, or special non-
       professional, non-technical schools, e.g.,
       Peace Corps., Armed Services, Primers

549   Citizen's Committees. Citizen participation

550   Advocate planning

       ACTION BY COMMUNITY

565   Direct improvement of conditions

569   Support of existing official agencies

571   Unofficial employment of experts, Cf. 875, 1540

573   Initiating and securing of legislation, Cf. 700

575   Public opinion

       SPECIAL ASPECTS

580   Village improvement movement, Cf. 5605

582   Garden city movement, Cf. 5350

584   Rural improvement movement. Landscape improve-
       ment

586   Women in city planning movement

587   Men in city planning movement

       LEGISLATION: UNITED STATES

700   General

700.1 Constitutional law

701   Executive: Presidential proclamations, Executive
       Orders, Speeches, etc.

702   Judicial

702.1 Court decisions

703   Congressional publications. Debates and Proceed-
       ings. Congressional Record

704   Documents and Reports (including Reports of
       Committees); Reports to Congress by Executive
       Branch

705   Hearings

706   Bills and resolutions

707   Laws and Statutes

707.3   Miscellaneous

708   State documents and codes, alphabetical by state

709   Bills, etc.

710   Laws and Statutes

711   Enabling legislation. Creation or empowering of administrative agents. Cf. 1520

712   Model Laws, etc.

713   Environmental agencies

714   City planning departments, commissions, etc. Cf. 1520

716   Authorities, etc.

      Creation of public properties, rights, etc.

720   General

721   Air rights

722   Acquisition of land and other privately-owned property. Eminent domain. Assessment laws, see 1580

      Condemnation of land, taking of land, etc.

724   Excess condemnation

728   Redistribution of land. "Lex Adickes". Zone condemnation

735   Creation of easements, rights-of-way, etc.

740   Acquisition of privately-owned utilities

750   Enforcing the city plan

755   Building lines and setbacks

757   MUNICIPAL LAW. Charters

758   Codes and Ordinances

759   Environmental control

760   CITY PLANNING LEGISLATION

765   Zoning legislation

766   Zoning administration

770   Platting legislation. Special. For regulative legislation relating to special subjects, see e.g., Districts, Streets, Buildings, Parks.

772   Esthetic regulation. Urban Design regulation

774   Architectural control

780 LEGISLATION: OTHER COUNTRIES. Subdivide by
      country.

    National

    State or province or other administrative unit

    Municipal

795 Other

    TECHNICAL PROCEDURE. PROFESSIONAL PRACTICE

800 General. City planning as a profession

805 General special. Announcements and brochures

810 Legislation. Regulation. Legal status

811 Professional examinations and registration

811.5 Relation to government

812 Official procedure

812.1   United States

812.2   Europe

812.3   Other

      METHODOLOGY. BASIC STUDIES AND SURVEYS

815 General. Urban analysis. Basic surveys

816 Statistics

817 Data and records

    Automation, Data processing, Documentation

    Information storage and retrieval

818 Cybernetics

819 Systems analysis. Operations research

819.5 Decision making

    Special classes

820   Topographic, etc.

821   Sanitary and health

822   Social, recreation. Education, cultural, etc.
      Cf. 1400

824 Legal and administrative. Cf. 1500

826 Economic and financial. Cf. 1545

    Base studies

830 Reports, tabulations, compilations, censuses,
      data banks, etc.

831 Forecasts

833 Mathematical models

834 Maps, plans, etc.

835 Symbols

836 Models

837 Programming, linear programming, game theory

838 Audio and visual media

    Films, Holographs, Remote sensing

    Photographs, etc.

    Aerial maps and surveys. Cf. 1244.

848 Criteria, standards, etc.

850 Comprehensive plans. Master plans

857 Planning programming budgeting systems

858 Estimates

859 Contracts and specifications

860 DIRECTION OR SUPERVISION OF CONSTRUCTION AND MAINTENANCE

    Cf. subhead Construction and maintenance under individual elements e.g., Streets, Parks

870 Technical procedure in special fields

875 CONSULTATION, COOPERATION AND FUNCTIONS OF EXPERTS

878 Charges. Cost of city planning studies

880 COMPETITIONS

    Material relating to special competitions may be classified by the subject of the competition, or grouped here.

STUDY AND TEACHING

    Cf. 548. This section 900 is for professional study and teaching.

900 General

905 General special

SUBJECT MATTER

910 General

912 Theory of city planning. Ekistics

914 Practice in design, economic, social and esthetic.

    Cf. 840, 1200

916 Elements of city plans. Factors and components.
    Cf. 1900

918 Construction and maintenance

920 Special contributory subjects

METHODS

930 General

935 Courses of study in universities, colleges,
    technical schools

940 Study in libraries, collections and exhibitions.
    Cf. 546

941 Discussion groups

942 Research

945 Observation and travel.

947   Study tours

950 Experience in offices of practitioners.
    Internships

SPECIAL COUNTRIES

960 United States

961 Canada

962 England

964 France

966 Germany

978 Other

SPECIAL SCHOOLS. UNIVERSITY OR COLLEGE DEPART-
MENTS. Including catalogues and bulletins.
Note: word "school" is used in the sense of
institution not in the sense, e.g. "school of
Sitte."

979 Institutions or organizations to promote learning

980 United States

982 England

984 France

986 Germany

998 Other

COMPOSITION OF CITY PLANS. PLANNING. REPLANNING

1200   General. General theory and principles of design

1201   General special

1205   Special Aspects. General considerations. Broad relations

1210   SOCIAL ASPECTS. SOCIAL SCIENCES, BEHAVIORAL SCIENCES. ETHICS. Cf. 1400 and subhead Social aspects under Elements.

1210.8   Minority and racial problems

1210.9   Religion

1210.10   Public welfare

1211   Family. Children. Youth

1212   Aged

1212.5   Handicapped

1213   Delinquency. Crime

1213.5   Police

1214   BEHAVIORAL SCIENCES. HUMAN ECOLOGY

1214.05   Psychological aspects

1214.06   Urban activity

1214.07   Right to privacy

1215   HEALTH AND SAFETY. PUBLIC HEALTH. Cf. 1445

1225   ECONOMIC ASPECTS. ECONOMIC BASE. POVERTY. EFFICIENCY OF THE COMMUNITY. MUNICIPAL GOVERNMENT

1225.5   Economic planning - Estimates

1228   Economic needs of the aged

ESTHETIC ASPECTS. CIVIC BEAUTY. CIVIC ART. CIVIC IMPROVEMENT. URBAN DESIGN. MUNICIPAL ART. GENERAL DECORATION OF CITIES. Cf. subhead Esthetic aspects under Elements, e.g., Buildings.

1235   General

1240   General special

1242   Organic beauty of city

1244   Birdseye views. Aerial views. Isometric views, et

1246   Influence of aviation on planning for appearance of city

1248 Silhouette, skyline
1250 Visual compositions seen from given points
        Views
1252 Vistas. Termini
1256 Color. Cf. 3517
1260 City at night. Lighting effects. Cf. 1476
1263 Vegetation. See 4815
1265 Water. Ornamental use of water. See also 3845

        HISTORIC ASPECTS
1270 General
1272 Truth to historic type; e.g., Old Sturbridge
        Village
1274 Preservation of individuality
1276 Preservation of historic features in cities.
        Cf. 4230
1279 Place names
1290 City planning of the future

        REPLANNING
1293 Replanning and reconstruction of destroyed cities.
        After Bombs, Earthquakes, Fire, Flood, Land-
        slides, etc.
1295 After-war planning

        FUNDAMENTAL CONDITIONS, EXISTENT AND PREDICTABLE
1300 General
1305 General special. Infrastructure
1308   Purposes and importance of data
1310   Sources

        CLIMATE, TOPOGRAPHY, SOIL, ETC. NATURAL ENVIRON-
        MENT. ECOLOGY
1320 General
1321 Geographic considerations
1322 Economic geography
1325 General special
        Climate. Cf. 5210
1330   General
1331   Microclimate
1332   Temperature

1334   Precipitation

1336   Winds

TOPOGRAPHY. CITY SITES. LOCATION
Cf. 1555, 5250, and subhead Topographic aspects,
under Elements, 1900

1340   General

1344   Topology

1345   General special

1346   Waste lands

1347   Artificial topography. Earthwork. Removal
of hills, filling of low or submerged areas.
Reclamation

Terracing

1348   Land forms

1350   General

1352   Plains, prairies, marshes. Cf. 5270

1354   Valleys. Cf. 5280

1356   Hills, slopes, hilltops. Cf. 5285, 5290

WATER BODIES, SHORES, WATERFRONTS
Cf. 2640, 4170

1360   General

1365   General special

1367   Use of shores, waterfronts, Cf. 2640, 4170

1368   Reclamation of shores, see also 1347.

1370   Coast, shores, estuaries. Of sea, arm of sea,
or large lake. Cf. 4181, 4182, 5255

1372   Islands. Cf. 4184, 5260

1373   Lakes and rivers

1374   Small lakes. Cf. 4182

1376   Rivers, streams. Cf. 2580, 4183, 5265

SOIL. GROUND WATER. INCLUDING SUBSOIL. Cf. 1557

1380   General

1382   Soil. Geological character. Types of soil. Soil
surveys. E.g., rock, gravel, sand, clay, peat,
loam. Cf. 1715, Agricultural districts, and
4800, Vegetation

1386   Ground water. Flow of underground water, water tab

12

1390   Other natural conditions

1392   Volcanoes, earthquakes, geysers, warm springs, etc.

POPULATION. SOCIAL CONDITIONS. MAN-MADE ENVIRONMENT

1400   General

1405   Demography

1406   Population studies, analysis, and estimates

1407   Statistics, vital statistics, and manner of life

1410   History of the city

1411   Economic considerations

1412   Social considerations

1415   Character, organization, and manner of life

1416   Cityward movement. Growth and evolution of cities. Ekistics

1417   Countryward movement. Urban-rural migration and development. Decentralization

1418   Relation to environment. City and country

1420   Distribution and density

1420.1   Congestion

1420.2   Daytime population

1421   Growth and changes

1422   Mobility and movement

1423   Migration

1425   Relocation

1426   Projections and forecasts

1427   Population planning. Birth control

1428   CONDITIONS AND STANDARD OF LIVING. COST. PRICES

1429   Income

1429.1   Income statistics

1429.4   Wages

1429.5   Bank deposits

HOUSING

1430	General
1430.01	Programs
1430.02	Societies
1430.03	Exhibitions
1430.05	Congresses
1430.1	Economic considerations
1430.2	Financial considerations (General, for specific methods of finance, see 1431)
1430.3	Esthetic considerations
1430.4	Social considerations. Public opinion polls
1430.41	Household activity
1430.42	Psychological considerations
1430.43	Geographic considerations
1430.45	Health and safety considerations
1430.5	Research. Study and Teaching
1430.51	History
1430.52	Publicity
1430.53	Study tours
1430.55	Surveys
1430.6	Technical procedure
1430.7	Terminology
1430.8	Statistics (other than cost, for which see 1433.1)
1430.9	Housing for special classes e.g., for the aged, handicapped
1430.93	Housing for single persons
1430.94	Housing for students
1430.95	Housing for national defense, i.e., industrial housing, etc.
1430.96	Priorities
1430.98	Housing, After war
1430.99	Housing, War-time conversion
1431	HOUSING FINANCE
1431.1	Programs
1431.2	Land acquisition
1431.3	Mortgages
1431.4	Subsidies

14

1431.45   Middle and low income housing
1431.5   Cooperative and co-partnership.   Condominiums
1431.55   Employees' housing
1431.6   Building and loan associations
1431.65   Self-help
1431.7   Limited dividend
1431.8   Housing by private enterprise
1431.82   Insurance company housing
1431.85   Public vs. Private
1431.9   Taxation; Tax exemption

1432   HOUSING: LEGISLATION
1432.1   Federal
1432.2   State
1432.3   Municipal; Housing codes.   Zoning
1432.35   Court decisions
1432.37   Model tenement legislation
1432.4   Housing: Administration
1432.45   Personnel
1432.5   Federal
1432.6   State
1432.65   Regional
1432.7   Municipal
1432.8   Rural
1432.9   Management of individual projects

1433   HOUSING: CONSTRUCTION AND MAINTENANCE
1433.01   Statistics
1433.02   Designs and plans
1433.05   Building materials
1433.06   Mechanical equipment.   For other utilities,
              see 1541
1433.1   Cost
1433.2   Labor problems
1433.3   Prefabricated houses; Industrialized housing
1433.39   Obsolescence
1433.4   Rehabilitation of existing housing

1433.5   Community facilities, including recreation

1433.6   Grounds: Planting, drives, etc.

1433.65 Relation to streets and highways

1433.7   Location of projects

1433.8   Slum clearance; Rehousing. Cf. 1613, 1704

1433.9   Standards

1434   HOME OWNERSHIP

1434.1   Housing shortages and Housing vacancies.
           Market and demand

1434.2   Rentals and rent control

1434.3   Temporary housing. Emergency housing

1434.35 Dormitories (College; Use NAC 3571.)

1434.4   Minority and racial problems

1434.5   Housing. Hot climates

1434.51 Housing. Cold climates

1434.6   Management. Tenancy, Landlord-tenant relations

1434.7   Rural housing

1434.8   Labor camps

1434.9   Trailers and tourist camps, motor courts. Mobile
           housing, for subdivision, see 3095

1434.92   Social considerations of trailers, etc.

1434.95   Trailer legislation and taxation

1435   INDUSTRIAL CONDITIONS; INDUSTRIAL SURVEYS

1436   Technology and science

1438   Employment and city planning. Unemployment.
           Manpower. Labor force. Public works

1442   Fuel supply

1443   Food supply; Markets; Milk supply, etc.

1445   PUBLIC HEALTH AND SAFETY

1445.1   Public health and safety areas

1445.2   Surveys

1445.3   Programs

1445.4   Rural programs

1445.5   Statistics

1445.6   Insurance

1445.7   Study and teaching

1447 Air and sunlight. Air pollution, smog, and their control

1448 Nuisances; Pollution and control

1449 Smoke prevention. Cf. 4854

1450 Dust prevention

1451 Noise prevention

1452 Drainage of land; Insect control

1454 Protection from floods. Flood control. Cf. 3800

1456 Water-supply. Cf. 2885, 4510

1456.5 Financial

1458 Water pollution and control

DISPOSAL OF WASTE

1460 General

1461 Salvage of waste. Recycling

1462 Water-borne

1464 Sewage. Cf. 2890, 4520

1466 Surface water. Cf. 2890

1470 Solid waste. Non-water-borne

1472 Garbage, refuse, rubbish, etc.
Dumps, incinerators, etc. Cf. 4538

1472.5 Sanitary landfill

1474 Street cleaning

1475 Snow and ice removal

1476 Lighting. Cf. 1260, 3870

1478 Fire protection. Fire prevention. Cf. 2652, 2888, 3540

1479 Conflagrations. Fires. Bombs. Nuclear destruction, etc.

1483 Disposal of the dead. Cf. 4480

1485 Other

1490 EDUCATION. Cf. 3570

1490.1 Public school systems

1495 RECREATION. Cf. 3575, 3728, 4000

1495.1 Congresses

1495.2 Publicity

1495.3   Study and teaching

1495.5   War-time

1495.7   Racial problems

1495.8   In industry

1495.9   For the aged

1496   Legislation

1496.5   Administration

1496.6   Financial considerations

1497 Leisure

1498 Standards for recreation

1499 Other

LEGAL AND ADMINISTRATIVE CONDITIONS

1500 General

1503 Metropolitan districts

1503.1   Administration

1503.2   Social considerations

1503.4   Economic considerations

1503.5   Financial considerations

1504 Megalopolis

1505 Legal: General. Cf. 700

1510 Laws relating to public property, rights, etc.

1515 Laws relating to private property, rights, etc.

1516 Laws relating to equal rights

ADMINISTRATIVE. Cf. 711, where laws relating to
      creation of administrative agents should go

1520 General. Municipal affairs. Municipal governmen
      City managers

1520.1   Annexation

1520.2   Consolidation

1521 Relation of Federal, State, and Local. Inter-
      governmental relations. Councils of government

1522 Federal administration

1523 State administration

1524 Metropolitan and county. City-county consolid-
      ation. Cf. with 1503

1524.5 Political science

1524.6 Politics and planning

PUBLIC AGENCIES

1525 General

1525.5 Authorities. Special districts

1526 General special

1527 Relation of Federal, State, and Municipal agencies. Cf. 711, 1590

1530 Existing. Governmental control. Federal government ownership. Cooperating specialized activities. City engineers' departments. Departments of public works, street departments, water and sewerage boards, park departments, harbor boards and port directors, etc. Environmental agencies

1531 Bureaucracy

1535 Specially created. City planning departments, city planning commissions, etc. Cf. 714

1535.1 Art commissions

1540 Public consultation of experts, official employment of experts. Cf. 875

1540.1 Private agencies

1541 Public service corporations. Public utilities

1541.1 Municipal ownership

1541.2 Nationalized

1541.3 Legislation related to highways

1541.4 Construction and maintenance, including cost

1541.5 Public services

ECONOMIC AND FINANCIAL CONDITIONS. RESOURCES

1545 General

1550 General. Base studies. Industrial surveys. Commerce

1555 Advantages or disadvantages of situation of city. Cf. 1340

1557 Natural resources. Soil, mineral resources, water-power, etc.

1559 Commercial and industrial opportunities

1563   LAND USE, URBAN
1563.1 Administration. Policies and theory
1563.5 Legislation
1563.6   Zoning. See 1620. Cf. 765
1564   Technical procedure
          Survey and maps
          Classification
1565   Resources
1566   Economic considerations
1566.1   Land values. Effect of improvements
1566.2   Appraisal
1566.3   Taxation
1566.4   Unearned increment
1566.5   Real estate
1566.6   Real estate business
1566.8 Land ownership. Tenure
1566.9 Public ownership
1567   Relation to environment and urban structure
1567.1   Conservation
1567.2   Ecology factors
1567.3   Space requirements
1567.4   Density of development
1567.5   Social considerations
1568   Vacant and undeveloped land
1568.5 Reserves: for specific uses or functions,
          e.g., open spaces 4000, etc.
1568.8   Transitional areas

        PUBLIC FINANCE. MUNICIPAL FINANCE
1570   General
1570.5   Budgets. Capital improvement programs
1571   Technical procedure
1572   Cost benefit analysis
1573   General special; Valuation
1573.5   Income and cost studies

Income and expenditure

1575 General

1576 From loans

1578 From bond issues

1580 From taxation and assessment, betterments,
Benefit assessments, assessment districts, etc.

1581 Nontaxing authority

1583 From excess condemnation and resale

1585 From franchises, etc.

1588 From municipally owned property and enterprises.
(Municipal forests, leases of city lands,
municipal operation of public utilities.)

1590 From federal or state grants. Government aid.
Federal aid, cf. 1527. Tax sharing

1592 Financial relation to municipalities

1593 Financial relation to public utilities

1594 From gifts and bequests, etc.

1595 Expenditures. Estimate and apportionment. Cost
of executing city plans

ORGANIZATION AND SUBDIVISION OF CITY AREA BY
DOMINANT FUNCTION. DISTRICTS. ZONING

1600 General

1605 General special

1607 Relative size of districts

1609 Control of undeveloped land

1610 Development of new areas. Extensions. Expansion
of city. Cf. 1200, 1800

1611 Obsolescence

1612 Replanning

URBAN RENEWAL. EFFECTS OF CHANGE IN TYPE OF
OCCUPANCY. BLIGHTED (GRAY) AREAS. REHABILITA-
TION. RELOCATION. DEPRESSED AREAS

1613 General

1613.01 Statistics

1613.02 Administration

1613.03 Technical procedure

1613.1 Neighborhood conservation

1613.2 Community development and renewal

1613.3 Financial considerations

1613.4 Social considerations

1613.5 Programs. Model cities. Slum clearance, See 1704

1613.9 Arguments against

1616 House moving. Moving buildings

1618 Relocation of cities

1619 Minority and racial problems

1620 Legislation. Zoning. Ordinances. Regulations.
Maps. City extensions.
(Zoning administration, 766; Zoning legislation,
765.)

1622 Rural zoning

1623 Zoning - Court decisions

1625 ADMINISTRATIVE DISTRICTS

1627 Civic centers. Community centers. Neighborhood
Centers. Building grouping

1628 Educational districts. Cultural centers

1629 Art centers

1629.1 Music centers

BUSINESS DISTRICTS. COMMERCIAL DISTRICTS.
INDUSTRIAL DISTRICTS. Cf. 3190

1630 General

1631 General special

1632 Research centers

1633 Relation to transportation facilities

1640 Density of development, intensiveness of
occupancy, general character of building
development.
Height, cf. 3480; Materials, cf. 3510;
Construction, cf. 3540, etc.

INDUSTRIAL DISTRICTS

1650 Manufacturing districts. Cf. 3195

1652 Mines

1653 Stone quarries and gravel pits

1655 BUSINESS DISTRICTS. COMMERCIAL DISTRICTS.
CENTRAL BUSINESS DISTRICTS

1657 Warehouse, shipping districts

1660   Market districts. Market centers, cf. 1443,
            2234, 3610

1665   Wholesale districts

1667   Financial districts, cf. 3600

1670   Retail districts. Shopping centers, cf. 3210,
            3600

1671 Ribbon development

RESIDENTIAL DISTRICTS. Cf. 2235, 3230, 3380, 3620

1675   General

1676   General special. Neighborhood units

1677   Density of development. Congestion. Intensive-
            ness of occupancy. Number of houses to acre

1678   Relation to business encroachment

1679   Relation to traffic, through-traffic, etc.

        Urban

1680   General

1681   General special

        Suburban. Suburbs
            Cf. 5331; Garden suburbs, 5350

1685   General. Geographical subdivision here, e.g.
            Forest Hills, N.Y.

1686   General special, e.g. Suburban commercial

1687 Relation of growth of suburbs to transportation
            facilities

1690 Special types

        Districts distinguished by predominant cost of
            residences

1694   General

1695   High-cost

1696   Medium-cost

1697   Low-cost. Workingmen's homes; Industrial
            housing

        Districts distinguished by predominant type of
            residence

1698   General

        Houses in-block

1700   General

1701   Single

23

1702	Apartments (high-class)
1703	Tenements
1704	Slums and slum clearance. Blighted (gray) areas. Depressed areas
1704.5	Barrios; Squatter communities
	Detached houses
1705	General
1706	Single
1707	Semi-detached
1708	Other

AGRICULTURAL DISTRICTS, AGRICULTURAL BELTS, FOREST BELTS. Cf. 3244

1715	General
1720	Agricultural belts
1723	Market-garden areas
1724	Allotment gardens
1725	Forest belts. See 4160, Forest reservations

RECREATION AREAS. Open rings. Green belts. Cf. 4000

1730	General. Distribution. Recreation centers. Cf. 4318
1731	General special
1733	Relation to transportation facilities

BOUNDARY AREAS. Boundaries

1745	General
1748	Approaches and entrances
1750	City boundaries. Cf. 3825
1753	TRANSITIONAL AREAS, e.g. Commercial encroaching on residential

ORGANIZATION AND SUBDIVISION OF CITY AREA INTO STREETS AND BLOCKS. Land subdivision in the larger sense. Street systems. Platting

1800	General
1805	General special. Relation to topography
1808	Legislation. Street system, 2070. Cf. 700

1810   Location of main thoroughfares.   Cf. 2170

1812   Determining centers, foci.   (Local centers, see
       1627)

1814   Determining connecting routes

1820   Location of minor streets.   Cf. 2220

      TYPES OF PLATS.   Cf. 5630

1830   General

      Formal.

1835   General

1837   Gridiron.   Cf. 5637

1839   Gridiron and diagonal.   Cf. 5639

1841   Radial and round-point.   Cf. 5641

1844   Other, e.g. Cul-de-sac

      Informal.

1845   General

1847   Rectilinear.   Cf. 5647

1849   Curvilinear.   Cf. 5649

1851   Composite.   Cf. 5651

      ELEMENTS OF CITY PLANS

1900   General.   Collective

      CHANNELS OF TRANSPORTATION.   Of persons, commodi-
      ties, power.   Ways, conduits, wires.   Utilities.
      Subsurface channels

2000   General.   Networks.   Modes

2005   General special.   Industrial transportation
      Transportation of industrial workers

2006   Commuting

2010   Special aspects.   Urban transportation

2011   Topographic

2012   Social

2013   Health and safety

      Comfort and convenience

2014   Economic.   Effect on land development

2015   Esthetic

2016	Historic
2020	Legislation
2025	Special professional considerations. Administration. Authorities
2026	Data
2027	Design
2028	Construction and maintenance. Civil engineering. Automation. Vehicles
2029	Cost
2030	Vertical transportation
2031	Market and demand
2032	Forecasting

STREETS, ROADS, FOOTWAYS, HIGHWAYS, VEHICLES

2050	General
2055	General special
2056	Street names
2056.5	Street numbering
2057	Influence of traffic on street-form, street plan, etc. Congestion of traffic. Cf. 2076
2057.2	Congresses
2057.5	Research
2058	Influence on streets of changes in means of transportation. Impact of motor traffic. Automobiles Cf. 2076.3; 2358
2058.1	Automobile dimensions. Statistics
2059	Automobile parking. Relation to buildings and building groups
2059.1	Meters
2059.2	Lots and off-street parking generally. Loading docks and/or areas for people or goods
2059.21	Underground parking and garages
2059.22	Shopping centers
2059.23	Universities and colleges
2059.25	Zoning
2059.3	Perimeter parking
2059.4	Buildings - public garages. Parking garages

2059.5   Administration (authorities, etc.)

2059.6   Financing

2060   Special aspects

2070   Legislation, including Acquisition by city

2073   Set backs

2074   Street widening. Cf. 2105

2075   Special professional considerations. Traffic
        engineering and design

2076   Street traffic

2076.1   Traffic surveys and censuses. Origin-destination.
          Inventory. Peak loads. Traffic flow

2076.11   Technical procedure

2076.15   Highway capacity

2076.2   Data on vehicles. Circulation

2076.3   Regulations. Traffic engineering, Traffic control,
          Automated control, legislation, enforcement, etc.

2076.32   Relation to planning, communities, highways, etc.
           In metropolitan areas

2076.33   Congestion

2076.34   Street marking and signals

2076.35   Speed

2076.36   Accidents and safety

2076.38   Pedestrians. Pedestrian circulation. Bicycles

2076.39   Delays

2076.4   Parking. Cf. 2059

2076.5   Parking problems

2078   Construction and maintenance

2079   Cost

2080   Design

2081   Bypass highways

2085   Form, straight or curved

2090   Orientation. Cf. 3060

2095   Length, continuity

2100   Gradient

2103   Treatment of steep gradients. Hillside streets

2105   Width. Cross section

2106 Special components

2107 Separate roadways. See, 2115, Multiple streets

2108 Walks. See 2252, Footways

2109 (Planting strips. Parking. Reservations.)
See 4875, Street planting, and 2382, Street
transit reservations

2110 Special topography

2115 Streets specially subdivided. Multiple streets

2116 Parked streets

2118 Streets with irrigation canals

2119 Double-deck streets, two-level streets;
Multi-level streets

SURFACE. PAVEMENTS

2120 General

2121 Special kinds, arranged alphabetically

2122 Gutters, curbs

2124 Drain inlets, manhole covers, etc.

2128 Crossings, Pedestrian islands, Traffic islands
Street intersections

2135 Junctions. Intersections

2136 Intersection of lines of traffic, avoidance of
collision points

2137 Vision clearance

2138 Viaducts. Overpasses. Underpasses. Grade
separation. Interchanges

2150 Proportion of street area to block area

RELATION TO BUILDINGS

2155 General

2157 Set-backs. Building lines. Legislation. See
also 2070

2159 Encroachments of buildings or structures, balconies, stoops, overhangs, marquees,
projections, etc. Sidewalk obstruction

2161 Arcades, colonnaded streets, covered streetways
and footways, galleries

2163 Relation to height of buildings. Cf. 3083, 3480

HIGHWAYS, THOROUGHFARES, MAJOR STREETS, URBAN
ARTERIAL HIGHWAYS, INTERURBAN HIGHWAYS

2170 General

2175 General special. Include here "motor roads,"
highways in cities

2180 Special forms, e.g. Divided highways

2181 Elevated highways. Depressed highways

2182 Radial

2183 Circumferential, peripheral

2184 Diagonal

2187 Ramps, approaches

2188 Other

SPECIAL USES. MULTIPLE USE

FOR BUSINESS TRAFFIC. TRUCK ROUTES. Cf. 4891

2195 General

2197 Traffic squares. Roundpoints. Traffic circles
Center strips. Cf. 4420

2199 Taxi stands

2201 One-way streets

FOR PLEASURE TRAFFIC. TOURWAYS. Cf. 4196, 4893

2205 General. Drives

2207 Formal. Boulevards, etc.

2209 Informal. Parkways, etc.

2210 Scenic highways

2211 Concourses

2212 Park roads

2213 Bridle paths

2214 Bicycle paths

2215 Off-road vehicles, snowmobiles

LOCAL STREETS. Cf. 1820

2220 General

2225 General special

SPECIAL USES

2230　For business. As frontage for business buildings,
　　　etc. Cf. 1630, 4891

2233　Business squares

2234　Market squares

　　　FOR RESIDENCE. RESIDENTIAL STREETS. Cf. 1675,
　　　4892

2235　General

2236　Urban

2237　Suburban

2238　Open space. Residential squares. Terraces.
　　　Courts

2240　For play: streets as playgrounds.

　　　Special forms

2242　Alleys. Service ways. Cf. 3181

2244　Private ways

2245　**Conveyor** belts

　　　FOOTWAYS

2250　General

2252　Sidewalks. Walks. Moving sidewalks. Overhead
　　　sidewalks

2253　Drives across sidewalks

2254　Independent footways

2256　Steps, ramps, etc.

2258　Promenades, malls, etc.

　　　Covered footways. See 2161

2262　Footbridges and tunnels. Underground pedestrian
　　　footways

　　　HIGHWAY BRIDGES AND TUNNELS. Cf. 3740

2270　General

2271　Bridges, Toll

2272　Special purposes to cross water, railroads,
　　　highways, etc.

2276　Approaches, ramps

2278　Draws

2282　Vertical transportation

2284　Subsidiary uses

2286   Bridges.   Culverts

2288   Tunnels

STREET FURNITURE.   Cf. 3860

2290   General

2292   Street nameplates.   Road guide signs

2294   Power lines and poles and wires.   Cf. 2386

2296   Police-boxes, fire-alarm boxes.   Mailboxes

2298   Toll booths

2304   Hydrants

2309   Street traffic furniture: Signal lights, etc.

2315   Street planting.   See 4875

2320   Street decoration for festivals.   Parades.
       Ceremonies

RAPID TRANSIT.   STREET RAILWAYS.   SUBWAYS.   MASS
TRANSPORTATION.   BUSES.   MONORAILS, AND OTHER
MODES.   Including interurban transit.   Cf. 1687,
1733, 2807

2350   General

2355   General special.   Relation to housing, planning,
       suburbs, etc.

2355.1 Administration.   Authorities

2355.2 Finance

2356   Relation to street.   Connections between transpor-
       tation lines, subway approaches

RAPID TRANSIT

2357   Obstruction of surface traffic by transit
       structures

2358   Buses.   Cf. 2058

2360   Special aspects

2370   Legislation

2375   Special professional considerations

2378   Passenger transportation

2379   Freight transportation

SURFACE TRANSIT

2380   General

2382   Street transit reservations.   Multiple use

31

2384 Tracks. Ways. Location, width, spacing, curves, etc.

2386 Power lines, underground cables, etc. Cf. **2294**

2390 Elevated transit, including bridges and viaducts. Cf 3740

2395 Elevated transit stations

2400 Subways, tunnels, tubes, underground transit

2405 Subway stations and station approaches. Subway entrances. Vertical transportation

2410 Shelters, waiting stations, transfer stations

2420 Transit terminals. Garages. Car-barns, yards

2430 Funicular railroads

RAILROADS. Cf. 2714, 5316

2450 General. Railway systems

2455 General special

2457 Electrification. Automation

2458 Government ownership

2460 Special aspects. Esthetic aspects. Planting. Improvement of station grounds, see 2485

2470 Legislation

2475 Special professional considerations

2478 Passenger transportation

2479 Freight transportation

2480 Stations. Cf. 3605. Material may be grouped und either number, according to point of view.

2483 Union stations. Terminals. Cf. 2785

2484 Tracks. Vehicles. High-speed, or other special forms

STATION PLACES. STATION SQUARES. STATION GROUND

2485 General

2486 Urban. Railroad planting

2487 Suburban

2488 Village

2490 Train yards

2493 Sidings

2495 Freight houses and yards

RIGHTS-OF-WAY
2500	General
2502	Through lines
2504	Belt lines
2505	Industrial railroads
2507	Local and light railroads
2510	Crossings
2512	At grade. Grade crossings
2513	Grade separations

RAILROAD BRIDGES AND TUNNELS. Cf. 3740
2515	General
2516	To cross land
2517	To cross water
2520	Special uses
2522	Freight tunnels
2524	Draws
2526	Vertical transportation
2528	Bridges
2529	Tunnels

WATERWAYS AND WATERFRONTS, COMMERCIAL. **Cf.** 5317
2550	General. Ports
2555	General special
2558	Recreational uses
2559	Marine structures
2560	Special aspects
2570	Legislation. Including port regulation
2571	Administration. Authorities
2575	Special professional considerations

RIVERS, CANALS. Cf. 1376, 5265
2580	General
2585	Channels
2588	Locks
2590	Banks
2595	Bridges. See also 3740

BAYS, HARBORS, BASINS

2600 General

2605 Channels and anchorages. Moorings. Location, marking, dredging, etc.

2608 Lighthouses

2610 Harbor lines, bulkhead lines, etc.

Protective works. Cf. 3800

2615   General

2617   Breakwaters, jetties, etc.

2619   Sea walls

2625 Defensive works. Cf. 3810

2630 Harbors and basins for special purposes. E.g. fishing fleet, yachting fleet, houseboats, marinas

WATERFRONTS. For recreational waterfronts, see 4170

2640 General

2645 General special. Administration

Special

2650 Capacity, frontage

2652 Fire protection. Cf. 1478

Docks, slips, etc.

2660   General

2665   Special. E.g. size

2670   Docking apparatus

2675   Ferry slips and ferries

WHARVES, PIERS, JETTIES, QUAYS, ETC. For recreation piers, see 4199

2680 General

2685 Special. Facilities. Construction length, etc.

2690 Administration quarters, including quarantine, Revenue Service, custom house, accommodation for employees

SPECIAL PROVISION FOR PASSENGERS. Cf. 2800

2695 General

2697 Landing stages

2699   Shelters, waiting places, etc.

2701   Areas for vehicles. Parking

2705   Hotels, motels, etc.

SPECIAL PROVISION FOR FREIGHT. Cf. 2820

2710   General. Facilities

2712   Freight and cargo handling apparatus

2714   Railroad lines. Cf. 2450

2716   Areas for vehicles. Parking. Loading. Trucking
     facilities

2718   Warehouses, sheds, transit sheds, storage
     Cf. 3605

2720   Areas for handling and storing special classes of
     freight

2722   Grain, grain elevators

2723   Lumber, coal, stone, gravel, etc., yards

2724   Oil, chemicals, explosives

2725   Perishable goods, cold storage goods

2729   Liquids. Other

2730   Storage areas. For roofed storage areas, see
     2718

2735   Shipyards. Drydocks

2740   Industrial areas, utilization of waterfront by
     manufacturing plants

2744   Shipbuilding plants

TERMINAL FACILITIES

2750   General

2755   General special. Administration

2760   Special aspects. For handicapped, etc.

2770   Legislation

2775   Special professional considerations

Types, by mode of transportation

2780   Transit. Buses. Interurban systems

2785   Railroads

2790   Waterways and waterfronts. See 2550

AIRPORTS. AIRPLANES, JETS, HELICOPTERS, ETC.
AERIAL TRANSPORTATION FACILITIES. HANGARS.
LANDING FIELDS

2795   General
2795.1   Congresses
2795.2   Location
2795.3   Transportation to and from airports
2795.4   Passenger facilities
2795.41   Baggage handling
2795.45   Hotels, motels
2796   Special
2796.1   Economic and financial aspects
2796.2   Effect on land values
2796.21   Effect on community
2796.22   Access; Approaches
2796.3   Lighting, heating
2796.4   Noise nuisance
2796.5   Freight. Cargo. Loading facilities
2796.6   Vertical takeoff/landing facilities
2797   Legislation
2797.5   Administration
2797.6   Zoning
2799   Seaplanes

TRANSPORTATION FACILITIES

TYPES, BY KIND OF TRAFFIC

PASSENGER

2800   General
2805   General special
2807   Relation to local transportation and rapid trans
          and other systems. Cf. 2350

FREIGHT AND FREIGHT HANDLING

2820   General
2825   General special
2827   Relation to markets. Cf. 1660
2828   Relation to industrial areas
2829   Transshipment. Relation to other systems. Free
          ports

UTILITIES. CONDUITS. WIRES

2850 General

2855 General special

2857 Relation to street

2860 Special aspects

2870 Legislation

2875 Special professional considerations

CONDUITS, PIPES, ETC.

2880 General. Subsurface utilities. Piping

2885 Water-supply and distribution, including aqueducts
Cf. 1456. For monumental aqueducts, see 3740

2888 Fire-protection water-supply. Cf. 1478

2890 Sewerage and surface drainage systems. Storm
sewers. Cf. 1462, 4520

2891 Finance

2892 Legislation

2895 Subsurface drainage systems

2900 Gas distribution systems

2902 Central heating systems

2905 Pneumatic tube systems

2910 Steam. Other

WIRES AND POWER LINES. Cf. 4856

2915 General

2920 General special

2921 Overhead wires

2922 Removal of overhead wires. Underground wires

2925 Electric service distribution

2926 Alarm systems

2930 Telephone and telegraph wires

2935 Radio and television, including cable, transmission

BLOCKS AND LOTS. LAND SUBDIVISION. PLANNED UNIT DEVELOPMENT. Cf. 3380. Put here general material relating to both blocks and lots, putting special material relating to one alone under Blocks or Lots.

3000 General

3005 General special

3010 Special aspects

3011 Topographic

3012 Social

3013 Health and safety

3014 Economic

3015 Esthetic

3016 Historic

3020 Legislation. Regulations. Restrictions. Standards. Cf. 1620. Zoning

3025 Special professional considerations

3026 Data

3027 Design

3028 Construction and maintenance

3029 Cost

SIZE, SHAPE, ORIENTATION, TOPOGRAPHY. ADAPTABILITY TO DEVELOPMENT. REDISTRIBUTION OF LAND. Cf. 3120, 3270

3040 General

3045 Size. Dimensions. Cf. 3125, 3275

3050 Shape. Proportions. Cluster

3060 Orientation. Cf. 2090

3065 Topography

3070 Relation to street. For relation of block area street area, see 2150

3071 Relation to public facilities

RELATION OF AREA TO BUILDINGS THEREON. DENSITY DEVELOPMENT

3075 General

3077 Proportion of built-over area

3079 Disposition of built-over area

3081 Building lines. See 2157

38

3083   Building heights. Cf. 1640, 3460, 3480

3087   Disposition of vacant land

3089   Open space, courts, gardens, etc. Cf. 2238, 4900

3091   Ways, passageways, alleys, etc. Walk ways

3095   Mobile homes subdivision. See also 1434.9

      BLOCKS

3100   General

3105   General special

3115   Special professional considerations

      SIZE, SHAPE, ORIENTATION, TOPOGRAPHY. ADAPTABILITY
        TO DEVELOPMENT

3120   General

3125   Size. Dimensions. Superblocks

3130   General

3131   Rectangular

3133   Tapering

3135   With one side or more curvilinear

3139   Other

3140   Orientation

3145   Topography

3150   Relation to other blocks

3151   Equality

3152   Dominance or subordination

3155   Relation to street

3156   Relation to public facilities

3160   Subdivision into lots

3163   Fluctuation in sizes of component lots

      RELATION OF AREA TO BUILDINGS THEREON

3165   General

3167   Proportion of built-over area

3169   Disposition of built-over area

3177   Disposition of vacant land

3179   Open space, courts, block interiors. Atrium
      houses. Patio houses. Garden apartments

3181   Ways, passageways, alleys, etc. Access to interiors. Walk ways. Cf. 2242

3183   Corner reservations

SPECIAL TYPES OF OCCUPANCY

BUSINESS. Cf. 1630

3190   General

3195   Manufacturing plants. Buildings and grounds. Cf. 3595

3197   Brick-yards, lumber-yards, tan-yards, stock-yard etc.

3197.5   Other industrial structures

3199   Recreation areas for employees

3200   Warehouses. Cf. 1657, 3605

3205   Office buildings. Cf. 3600

3210   Retail shops and stores, Commercial structures Cf. 1670, 3600

3220   Other

RESIDENCE. Cf. 1675, 3380, 3620

3230   General

3235   Houses in-block. Cf. 1700, 3635

3240   Detached houses. Cf. 1705, 3650

3241   Cluster

3244   Agriculture. See 1715

3245   Recreation. See also 4000

LOTS

3250   General

3255   General special

3265   Special professional considerations

3269   Cost

SIZE, SHAPE, ORIENTATION, TOPOGRAPHY. ADAPTABILITY TO DEVELOPMENT

3270   General

3275   Size. Dimensions

Shape. Proportions

3280 General

3281 Shape

3282   Rectangular

3284   Unusual shapes

3285 Proportions

3286   Oblong

3289   Other

3290 Orientation

3293 Topography

3295 Hillside lots

3296 Waterfront lots

3300 Relation of lots to other lots

3304 Treatment of lot boundaries. Walls, fences, hedges. Cf. 3825

RELATION TO STREET

3305 General

3306 General special

3308 Corner lots. Cf. 3183

3310 Frontage

3311 Depth

3312 Grade

3313 Relation to public facilities

RELATION OF AREA TO BUILDINGS THEREON

3315 General

3317 Proportion of built-over area

3319 Disposition of built-over area

3327 Disposition of vacant land

3329 Gardens. See also 4900

3334 Other

RESIDENTIAL. LAND SUBDIVISION FOR RESIDENCES
Cf. 1675, 3230, 3620

3380 General

3385 Large estates

3390 Suburban places

3395 Building lots. House lots

STRUCTURES

3400   General
3405   General special. E.g. War conditions
3405.1 Building statistics
3410   Special aspects
3415   Esthetic
3416   Historic
3417   Conservation and restoration
3419   Other
3425   Special professional considerations
3430   Topography

BUILDINGS

3440   General
3445   General special
3448   Relation to surroundings.   Economic impact.
         Cf. 4550, 4600
3450   Special aspects
3452   Social
3453   Health and safety
3455   Esthetic
         General effect of style, scale, etc.   Consiste
3456   Historic
3457   Conservation and restoration

3460   LEGISLATION
         Building laws, Building codes. Building heigh
           Cf. 1620, Zoning; 2070, 2157, Building lines
           In general. Cf. 700
3465   Special professional considerations
3466   Data
3467   Designs and plans
3467.3 Handbooks
3468   Construction and maintenance
3469   Finance. Cost
3470   Orientation
3475   Relation to climate
3480   Size. Height. Cf. 2163, 3083

3489   High-rise building. Skyscrapers. Cf. 5660

3490   Style, architectural. Cf. 5690

3500   Special elements

3502   Domes, spires, towers, etc.

3503   Towers for broadcasting, etc.

3504   Roofs, chimneys, etc.

3506   Walls, doors, windows, etc.

3508   Porches, etc.

3509   Architectural details

3509.2 Out-buildings. Garages, etc.

3509.5 Substructures

BUILDING MATERIALS. Cf. 1640, 5680

3510   General

3515   General special

3517   Color. Cf. 1256

3521   Wood

3523   Brick and tile

3524   Stone. Masonry

3526   Concrete. Cement

3527   Reinforced concrete

3528   Iron and steel. Other Metals

3530   Decoration and ornament. Ironwork, lattice work.
       Special surface treatment. Tiles, stucco,
       plaster, plastic, etc. Concrete, etc.

TYPES OF CONSTRUCTION

3540   General

3541   Fire Insurance

3542   Fire-resistive. Cf. 1478

3543   Systems of fire-proofing

3544   Combustible

3545   Bomb proof construction, bomb resistant

3546   Structures for nuclear power

3547   Prefabrication. Industrialized building

3548   Geodesic domes. Pneumatic structures, etc.

3549 Portable

3550 Mechanical equipment

BUILDINGS FOR SPECIAL USES

3560 General. Collective

3563 Public buildings

Including federal, state, and municipal buildir

3565 Administration

Including capitols, city halls, courthouses, e

3568 Special municipal services

Including pumping stations, plants for water
treatment and distribution, water towers,
standpipes, power plants (including nuclear)
central heating plants, gas tanks, fire
stations, police stations, prisons, jails.
Cf. 4500. Open space devoted to operation
of special municipal services. Etc.

3570 EDUCATIONAL BUILDINGS. SCHOOLS, LIBRARIES,
MUSEUMS, ETC.

3570.1 Administration

3570.2 Legislation

3570.3 Finance

3570.5 Location

3570.55 Regional schools

3570.7 Statistics

3571 COLLEGES; HIGHER EDUCATION BUILDINGS; UNIVERSITII
COMMUNITY COLLEGES. CAMPUSES

3571.5 Relation to Community

3571.6 Higher education city planning considerations

3572 LIBRARIES

3573 CAMPS

3575 BUILDINGS FOR RECREATION; RECREATION CENTER
BUILDINGS. RECREATION CLUBS. OPERA HOUSES,
THEATERS, AUDITORIUMS. Cf. 3728

3578 NEIGHBORHOOD CENTERS

3580 HEALTH CENTERS. WELFARE CENTERS. PUBLIC BATHS,
GYMNASIA, ETC.

3585   HOSPITALS, ASYLUMS, ETC.

3588   DAY NURSERIES.   CHILD CARE

3590   RELIGIOUS BUILDINGS

3595   BUILDINGS FOR MANUFACTURING.   FACTORIES, MILLS,
        BREWERIES, ETC.

3600   BUILDINGS FOR BUSINESS AND COMMERCE.   SHOPS AND
        STORES, OFFICE BUILDINGS, BANKS, ETC.   Cf. 3205,
        3210

3605   BUILDINGS FOR TRANSPORTATION AND STORAGE.   RAILROAD
        STATIONS.   Cf. 2480; Warehouses, Cf. 1657, 2718,
        3200, etc.

3608   PUBLIC GARAGES

3610   MARKETS.   Cf. 1660

3615   COMMUNITY KITCHENS

3618   HOTELS, MOTELS, CLUBS, ETC.

3619   LODGING AND BOARDING HOUSES

        RESIDENCES
3620   General
3625   General special
3628   Terrace treatment
3630   Special types
3631   High-cost
3632   Medium-cost
3633   Low-cost

        HOUSES IN-BLOCK.   Cf. 1700, 3235
3635   General
3636   Single.   Row houses.   Group or court, atrium,
        patio houses
3637   High-cost
3638   Medium-cost
3639   Low-cost

3641 Multiple. Apartments. Garden apartments
3642   High-cost
3642.1   High rise
3643   Medium-cost. Cf. 1696
3644   Low-cost. Tenements. Cf. 1697, 1703

DETACHED HOUSES

3650 General
3651 Single
3652   High-cost
3653   Medium-cost
3654   Low-cost; Cottages
3656 Semi-detached
3658   Medium-cost
3659   Low-cost
3669 Other

MINOR BUILDINGS

3670 General
3672 Garages
3675 Shelters, pavilions. Utility buildings. Cf. 241
    4137, 4345
3677 Public comfort stations
3681 Bandstands, etc.
3684 Booths, street stands. Roadside stands. Informa
    tion centers
3685 Automobile service stations
3687 Greenhouses. Cf. 4545
3689 Other

BUILDING GROUPS. Cf. 4550

3700 General
3705 General special
3710 Design. Of groups of buildings and their inter-
    relation. For design of buildings individually
    see 3440
3715 Building groups for special uses
3717 Public buildings

3720 Administrative, civic centers. Cf. 1627, 3565, 4570

3721 Business and commercial

3722 Educational, campus planning, etc. Cf. 3570

3724 Exposition groups. Cf. 4585

3728 Recreational, etc. Cf. 3575

3738 Other

3739 MONUMENTAL WATERFRONTS

BRIDGES. VIADUCTS. AQUEDUCTS. Cf. 2138, 2390, 2885. General material on bridges and viaducts considered as structures, e.g. bridge design - architectural and engineering considerations

3740 General

3745 General special

3760 Legislation

3765 Special professional considerations

3770 Design

3771 Covered bridges

3780 Materials

3786 Toll booths

3790 Bridges and viaducts for special uses. See the special uses: 2270, Highway bridges; 2262, Footbridges; 2390, Transit bridges; 2515, Railroad bridges

3800 DAMS. DIKES. LEVEES. CANALS AND LOCKS. Cf. 1454, 2615

DEFENSIVE WORKS

3805 Defense planning. Cf. 1480, 2625

3806 Defense councils

3807 Decentralization for defense

3810 General. Civil defense

3810.5 Nuclear blasts and buildings
Bomb proof construction, see 3545

3811 Air raid shelters

3812 Fortifications. Forts

3813 Camouflage

3814 Blackouts

3815 City walls. City gates

MINOR STRUCTURES. Cf. 3670, Minor buildings

3820 General

3825 Walls, fences, gates, etc. Boundary structures.
      Cf. 3304

3830 Monuments, monumental arches, obelisks, etc.
      Monumental sculpture

3840 Statues, including monumental statues, sculpture

3845 Fountains, basins, etc.

3849 Drinking fountains, troughs. Wells

3855 Clocks

3857 Flagpoles, flagstaffs

3860 Street and park furniture. Seats, waste cans,
      etc. Cf. 2290, Street furniture, and 4141,
      Park furniture

3870 Lighting fixtures, lamp-posts, electroliers, etc.
      Cf. 1476

3872 City scales

3875 Illuminated signs, etc.

3878 Kiosks. Advertising kiosks

3880 Billboards. Posters. Billboard nuisance

3882 Shop signs. Commercial street signs

3890 Other

OPEN SPACES, PUBLIC AND QUASI-PUBLIC, OTHER THAN
FOR TRAFFIC. Cf. 1730

4000 General

4005 General special

4010 Special aspects

4011   Topographic

4011.1 Ecologic

4012   Social

4013   Health and safety

4014   Economic

4015   Open spaces as obstructions to traffic

4016   Effect of open spaces on land values. Cf.
          1566.1

4017 Acquisition

4020　Esthetic

4021　Preservation of natural landscape.

4022　Types of treatment, formal and informal

4025　Historic.　Memorial areas and parks

4026　Conservation.　Relation to environment

4030　Legislation

4035　Special professional considerations

PARK SYSTEMS AND OPEN SPACES

4040　General

4050　Legislation

4052　Administration

4052.3　Finance

4055　Special professional considerations

4056　Design

4057　Conservation

4058　Construction and maintenance

4058.3　Service facilities.　Equipment

4060　Park systems for special types of cities

4085　　Industrial cities

4090　　New towns

PARKS AND RESERVATIONS

4100　General

4105　General special

4106　Encroachments on public parks.　Buildings in parks, e.g. Museums

4108　Private concessions

4120　Legislation.　Park regulations

4121　Acquisition of land.　Cf. 722

4123　Administration and park management

4125　Special professional considerations

4126　Data

4127　Design

4128　Construction and maintenance

4129　Cost

PROVISION FOR RECREATION. Comfort and pleasure
Facilities and Equipment

4135 General

4136 Camps

4137 Resting places, shelters, utility structures,
      pavilions, etc. Cf. 3675

4139 Restaurants and refreshment facilities

4141 Park furniture. Cf. 3860

4143 Park lighting

4145 Park roads. See also 2212
      RESERVATIONS

4150 General

4155 General special

4158 Open rings. Green belts. Cf. 1730

4160 FOREST AND WATER-SUPPLY RESERVATIONS

4161 Administration. Management. Foresters

4162 Forest

4165 Water-supply

4166   Watersheds

4168   Reservoirs

SHORE RESERVATIONS. RECREATIONAL WATERFRONTS

4170 General

4175 General special

4177   Combination with commercial utilization

4179 Abuse of shores. Pollution
      Special situations

4181 Seashore. Marine parks. Cf. 1370

4182 Lake. Cf. 1370, 1374

4183 River. Cf. 1376

4184 Island. Cf. 1372

4190 Types of treatment, formal and informal

4195 Provision for special forms of recreation

4196 Drives, shore boulevards

4197 Promenades, embankments. Cf. 2258

4199 Recreation piers

4201   Bathing beaches

4203   Boating facilities. Marinas

4205   Winter-sport facilities. Snowmobiles

4210   Reservoir reservations, not primarily parks
       Cf. 4168, 4510

4220   Summit reservations, outlooks, etc. Hills and
       mountains. Cf. 1356

4224   Places containing special archaeologic, natural and
       historic features

4225   Places containing special natural features. Cf.
       4021

4226   Conservation and relation to environment

4230   Places of special archaeologic and historic interest
       Cf. 1276

4231   Scenic reservations

4240   Large parks. Country parks

4245   Small parks, commons, garden squares, neighborhood
       parks. Village greens. Pocket parks

4250   General

4265   Botanical gardens

4270   Zoological parks. Zoos

4274   Other

4275   Open-air theaters. Settings for pageants.
       Drive-in theaters

4280   Open-air concert and beer gardens. Music shells

4290   Amusement parks. Street transit parks

4295   Fair grounds

4298   Country clubs

       PLAYGROUNDS, ATHLETIC FIELDS. AREAS FOR SPORTS
       AND GAMES

4300   General

       PLAYGROUNDS

4310   General

4315   General special

4316   Distribution of playgrounds

4317.2 Neighborhood playgrounds

4317.3 Play lots for the very young

51

4318   As social centers

4319   School playgrounds

4330   Legislation

4333   Administration and management

4335   Special professional considerations

4336   Data

4337   Design

4337.2 Finance

4338   Construction and maintenance

4339   Cost

4340   Areas for games and sports

4343   Lighting

4345   Buildings for sports and games, shelter and
       facilities, utilities, etc. Cf. 3675

4350   Swimming pools, wading pools. Equipment

4355   Apparatus

4360   Planting. See also 4945

4370   Athletic fields, ball grounds, basketball, tennis
       courts, etc.

4375   Stadiums

4380   Race tracks. Speedways

4384   Aviation grounds. Aerodromes

4385   Provision for other special sports including
       golf courses, skating rinks, etc.

4395   DRILL GROUNDS

       SQUARES

4400   General

4405   General special. History

4415   Special professional considerations

4416   Design

4420   Traffic. See 2197

4423   Station places. Station squares. See 2485

4425   Market places. Market squares. Cf. 1660

4430   Congregating places, forum

4435   Architectural, Monumental. Cf. 3715, 4575

4440 Business. See 2233

4445 Residential. See 2238

4450 Garden. See 4245

4460 Camping grounds. Trailer camps, etc.

CEMETERIES

4480 General. Cf. 1483

4485 General special. Crematories

4495 Special professional considerations

OPEN SPACES DEVOTED TO SPECIAL MUNICIPAL SERVICES
Location and design, including location of
buildings in area. For Buildings, see 3568

4500 General

4501 General special

4505 Special professional considerations

4510 Water-supply areas. Including reservoirs, basins,
filtration plants. Cf. 1456, 4160, 4210

4520 Sewage disposal areas. Including treatment plants
Cf. 1464

4538 Refuse disposal facilities. Municipal dumps
Cf. 1472

4540 Municipal garages and other buildings and areas
Yards, stables, for use of municipal departments
City yards. Areas for storage of municipal
equipment and vehicles. E.g. equipment for
street cleaning, waste disposal, snow and ice
removal, etc.

4545 Municipal nurseries. Greenhouses. Cf. 3687

4549 Other

GROUNDS OF BUILDING GROUPS. Cf. 3700

4550 General

4555 General special

4565 Special professional considerations
Special types

4570 Civic centers. See 1627, 3720

4575 Architectural and monumental squares. See 4435

4585 Exposition grounds. See also 3724

GROUNDS OF SINGLE BUILDINGS. Cf. 3560

4600 General

4605 General special

4615 Special professional considerations

4620 Special types. Cf. 3560, Buildings for special uses

VEGETATION

4800 General

4805 General special

4810 Special aspects

4811 Climate

4813 Health and safety

4814 Economic

4815 Esthetic

4820 Legislation

4830 Vegetation types or plant communities
    Vegetation suitable for urban conditions

4835 Design. Planting design
    Construction and maintenance

4840 General

4842 Cost

4844 Soil preparation and cultivation. Irrigation. Drainage. Cf. 1380

4846 Protection. Tree guards, railings, copings, etc.
    Prevention and mitigation of adverse conditions and pollution of environment

4850 General

4852 Insect pests, spraying, etc.

4854 Smoke. Cf. 1449

4856 Power lines, wires. Cf. 2915

4858 Underground gas-leaks

SPECIAL FORMS. HORTICULTURAL MATERIALS

4859 General

4860 Trees. Cf. 4885

4861 Shrubs. Cf. 4886

4862 Herbaceous plants. Cf. 4887

4863   Turf. Cf. 4888

4864   Artificial materials

4870   Special uses

STREET PLANTING. ROADSIDE IMPROVEMENT. Cf. 2315

4875   General. Screening

4880   General special

4882   Selection of trees, etc., for streets

4885   Trees. Cf. 4860

4886   Shrubs. Cf. 4861

4887   Flower beds. Cf. 4862

4888   Turf strips. Cf. 4863

4889   Artificial materials

       Special uses

4891   Business streets. Cf. 2195

4892   Residential streets. Cf. 2235

4893   Parkways, boulevards. Cf. 2207

LOT PLANTING

4900   General. Yards. Screening. Cf. 3329

4901   Dooryard gardens

4902   Backyard gardens

4903   Courtyard gardens. Terraces, patios, cf. 3089

4905   Vacant lot gardens

4907   School gardens

4909   Rock gardens. Lawns. Fruit trees. Vegetable gardens. Etc.

BUILDING DECORATION

4910   General

4911   Foundation planting

4912   Vines

4914   Window gardens, window boxes, balcony gardens

4916   Plants (e.g. bay trees) in tubs, boxes, pots

4919   Roof and penthouse gardens

PLANTING OF OPEN SPACES. Cf. 4000

4930   General

4935   Parks

4937   Green belts

4940   Public gardens.

4945   Playgrounds. Cf. 4360

5000   OTHER ELEMENTS

TYPES OF CITY PLANS. Individual cities go with
6800, City planning, by special countries and
cities arranged geographically

5200   General

5205   General special

TYPES DISTINGUISHED BY CLIMATE. Cf. 1330

5210   General

5215   Temperate

5220   Hot. Tropic

5225   Cold. Arctic

5230   TYPES DISTINGUISHED BY TYPES OF POPULATION, RACES,
NATIONALITIES. Cf. 1400

TYPES DISTINGUISHED BY RELATION TO TOPOGRAPHY.
Cf. 1340

5250   General

5255   Coast or shore cities. Cities on marshes.
Cf. 1370

5260   Island cities. Floating cities. Cities on water.
Cf. 1372

5261   Underwater communities and cities

5265   River cities. Cf. 1376, 2580

5270   Cities on plains. Cf. 1352

5280   Cities in valleys. Cf. 1354

5285   Cities on sloping sites, hillsides. Mountain
villages, etc. Cf. 1356

5290   Hilltop cities. Cf. 1356

TYPES DISTINGUISHED BY DOMINANT FUNCTION

5300   General

5305   Governmental. Capital cities

5309   Bastides

5310   Military and naval. Cantonments

5311   Military

5312   Air force bases

5313   Naval

  5314   Evacuation camps
5314.1   Refugee camps
5314.2   Migratory settlements
          COMMERCIAL
  5315   General
5315.2   Trade centers
  5316   Railroad centers. Cf. 2450
  5317   Ports. Cf. 2550
  5319   Other
          INDUSTRIAL. Cf. 1650, 4085
  5320   General
  5321   Manufacturing
5321.4   War industries
5321.5   Nuclear work
  5322   Mining
  5323   Labor and construction camps
  5324   Other
5324.5   CENTRAL PLACE THEORY
5324.51   Central places
  5325   EDUCATIONAL. University cities
  5330   RESIDENTIAL. Cf. 1675
  5331   Suburban cities and towns. Cf. 1685, Suburban
            districts
  5333   Resorts, health and pleasure
  5334   Institutional homes
  5340   NEW CITIES; NEW COMMUNITIES
5340.1   Administration
5340.2   Finance
5340.3   Legislation
5340.4   Economic considerations
5340.5   Social considerations

5340.6	Relation to environment
5345	Satellite towns
5347	Company towns
5350	GARDEN CITIES. GARDEN SUBURBS. GARDEN VILLAGES. Cf. 582, Garden City literature may be collected here with geographic arrangement; or local material may be put with 6800, City planning by special countries and cities
5355	Garden cities and villages for disabled or handi-capped
5360	Agricultural colonies or settlements
5361	Rural communities. Cf. 584
5370	UTOPIAS. IDEAL TYPES, ETC.
5375	Religious and mission towns
5380	Other towns

TYPES DISTINGUISHED BY SIZE OF CITY. For metropolitan districts, See 1503

5600	General
5605	Villages. To 2500 inhabitants. Cf. 580. Village improvement literature may be collected here.
5610	Small: 2500 - 10,000
5615	Medium: 10,000 - 50,000
5620	Large: 50,000 - 100,000
5625	Larger: 100,000 - 1,000,000
5626	Largest: 1,000,000 - 3,000,000
5627	Megalopolis: 3,000,000 or more
5629	Ghost towns, Deserted cities
5629.5	Boom towns

TYPES DISTINGUISHED BY STYLE OF CITY PLAN OR DOMINANT TYPES OF PLAT

5630	General. Cf. 1800
5635	Linear
5637	Gridiron
5639	Gridiron and diagonal
5641	Radial and round-point
5645	Circular
5647	Rectilinear

5649 Curvilinear

5651 Composite

5652 Other

5660 Dominant height of construction. Vertical cities.
   Skyscraper cities. High-rise buildings. Cf.
   3480

5680 Dominant building materials. Cf. 3510

5690 Dominant architectural style. Cf. 3490

6800 CITY PLANNING, BY SPECIAL COUNTRIES AND CITIES:
   Arranged geographically. See Geographical
   table. The Table may be used in two ways,
   either by deriving numbers based on 6800,
   e.g. Boston is 6827, or by adding g to the
   classification number, e.g. a Shopping center in Boston, 1670g27.

7000 GENERAL WORKS. PLANNING THEORY
7001 Technology and science related to planning

7010 COUNTY PLANNING
7010.1 Statistics
7010.2 Legislation. Cf. 700
7010.3 Administration
7011 Commissions
7011.5 Societies
7012 Technical procedure
7015 Reports and studies, individual counties
      English county plans use 6887.

7030 REGIONAL PLANNING, OTHER THAN METROPOLITAN
7030.1 Legislation. Cf. 700
7030.2 Interstate compacts
7030.5 Administration
7031 Economic considerations. Regional accounts
7031.1 Commissions
7032 Regional science
7033 Infrastructure
7034 Growth and change
7035 Reports and studies, individual regions
7035.1   Administration of individual regions
7035.5   Underdeveloped areas
7043 Corridor development

7050 STATE PLANNING
7051 Definition
7051.2 Legislation. Cf. 700
7052 Commissions
7053 Agencies
7053.5 Societies
7054 Financial
7055 Reports and studies, individual states,
    provinces, etc.

7070 NATIONAL PLANNING

7071 Legislation. Cf. 700

7075 Reports and studies

7080 National boundaries

7090 WORLD PLANNING. World centers and cities

7091 International relations. United Nations

7097 Outer space

7097.1 Space stations

7100 UNDERLYING FACTORS

ENVIRONMENT. ECOSYSTEM. ANALYSIS. STUDIES

7140 General

7140.2 Congresses

7141 Legislation. See also Cf. 700

7142 Administration

7143 Protection and conservation

7143.2 Programs

7143.5 Environmental design

7144 International cooperation

7145 Citizen participation, Cf. 549

7146 Study and teaching, Cf. 900

7147 Technology and science related to environment

7149 Pollution and control. Including radiation

7150 Impact on man. Human ecology

7150.1 Social considerations

7150.2 Economic considerations

7150.3 Financial considerations

7150.4 Budgets

7150.5 Private activity

7155 Standards. Quality of life, or air, etc.

7156 Forecasts

7159 ATMOSPHERIC SCIENCES

7160 Climate

7161 Climate and planning

7170   EARTH SCIENCES

7171   Geology

7172   Geography and topography

7173   Economic geography

7174   Ecology

        CONSERVATION

7180   General

7180.2 Resources

7180.3 Legislation. Cf. 700

7180.4 Administration

7185   International considerations

7186   Programs

7186.2 Political aspects

7186.3 Private aspects

7187   Consumption

7188   Future considerations and forecasts

7200   SOCIAL AND ECONOMIC FACTORS

7250   Population. See also 1400, 8600

7260   Pattern or distribution; Decentralization,
          Residential or Industrial

7270   Characteristics

7275   Health and welfare

7280   Economic conditions

7280.5 Statistics

7280.7 Input-output analysis

7282   Financial conditions and programs

7285   Taxation

        LAND USE AND CONSERVATION

7320   General. **Land resources**

7321   Legislation. Cf. 700

7322   Administration. Policies and theory

7322.1 Zoning, Cf. 765

7323   Technical procedure

7324   Surveys and maps

7325   Classification

7330   Resources
7330.1 Woodlands
7330.2 Grasslands
7330.3 Deserts
7330.4 Arctic regions
7330.5 Tropic regions
7335   Vacant and undeveloped land
7340   Economic considerations
7341   Land values
7342   Density of development
7343   Land ownership. Tenure
7350   Relation to environment
7351   Ecology
7352   Conservation
7353   Space requirements
7355   Reserves for open space. For specific uses or
        functions, see Agriculture, Cf. 7400, etc.
7359   Waste disposal
7360   Social considerations
7365   Esthetic considerations
7370   Rural areas and planning
7372   Other transitional areas

7400   AGRICULTURE, FARMING
7400.1 Statistics
7400.2 Legislation. Cf. 700
7400.3 Economic considerations. Government aid
7400.5 Social considerations
7402   Soil
7405   Farm ownership and tenancy
7406   Cooperative farms
7407   Part-time farming
7408   Farm taxation
7410   Grasslands. Cropping
7440   Animal husbandry
7445   Orchards

7450   Grazing
7460   Marginal uses
7465   Retirement of land

7500   LAND RECLAMATION
7501   Economic considerations
7502   Legislation
7540   Irrigation
7550   Land drainage
7560   Erosion and control
7561   Legislation
7562   Administration
7565   Water
7570   Wind
7575   Strip mining
7577   Other

7600   FORESTS AND FORESTRY. WOODLANDS
7601   Statistics
7601.5 Legislation
7602   Administration. Foresters
7603   Economic considerations
7604   Forest fires
7605   Reforestation
7606   Memorial forests
7608   Municipal forests
7609   County forests
7610   State forests
7612   Legislation
7620   National forests
7621   Legislation
7622   Encroachments
7625   Recreational use
7630   Private

7650	RECREATION
7651	Legislation
7652	Administration
7655	Recreation industry
7665	Structures. Facilities
7670	Camping and facilities
7675	PARKS
7676	Holiday villages
7677	REGIONAL PARKS
7678	COUNTY PARKS
7680	STATE PARKS
7680.1	State park systems
7680.5	Statistics
7681	Legislation
7681.05	Administration
7682	Construction and maintenance
7683	Financial considerations
7684	Use
7685	NATIONAL PARKS
7686	Legislation
7686.5	Administration
7687	Design
7687.5	Use
7688	Encroachments
7689	Statistics
7690	Structures. Facilities
7691	Camping and facilities
7694	INTERNATIONAL PARKS
7695	PLAY AREAS (GAMES AND ATHLETICS)
7696	Baseball
7697	Tennis
7698	Golf
7699	Other
7700	Water sports and areas
7701	Boating and marinas

7701.5   Legislation
  7702   Bathing, Beaches
  7704   Picnicking
  7706   Amusement areas
  7707   Fair grounds
  7708   Race tracks
  7709   Winter sports
7709.1   Snowmobiles
  7710   Skiing
  7712   Hiking. Trails
  7715   Riding. Trails. Polo fields

  7720   SCENIC AREAS AND PRESERVATION
  7721   Ocean. Seashore
  7722   Lake
  7723   Marsh
  7724   River
7724.5   Waterfall
  7725   Gorge
  7726   Valley
  7727   Mountain
7727.5   Cliff
  7728   Outlooks. Roadside parks
  7729   Wilderness

  7730   GEOLOGIC INTEREST
  7732   Minerals
  7733   Caves and other natural formations

  7735   BOTANIC INTEREST

  7740   WILDLIFE AREAS
7740.1   Congresses
7740.5   Legislation
7740.6   Administration
  7741   Bird sanctuaries, etc.
  7742   Hunting
  7743   Shooting grounds

7744 Game farms and preserves

7746 Fishing

7747 Fishing areas

7748 Fish preserves

7749 Fish hatcheries

7750 HISTORIC AND ARCHAEOLOGIC AREAS. NATIONAL
       MONUMENTS

7751 Forts

7752 Public buildings

7753 Religious institutions

7754 Houses and grounds

7756 Cemeteries

7758 Indian relics. Prehistoric artifacts

7760 Sites of events

7761 Other

7800 RESERVES FOR OTHER SPECIFIC PURPOSES

7820 Indian

7830 Defense

7832 State

7834 National

7850 MINING AND EXTRACTION

7850.1 Mining pits

7850.5 Statistics

7880 Fuels

7890 Metals

7900 Fertilizers and chemicals

7910 Sand. Clay. Gravel

7911 Stone quarries and gravel pits

7920 Other minerals

7921 Oil fields

7949   OCEANIC SCIENCES

7950   WATER RESOURCES AND CONSERVATION
       See also 7500. For Hydroelectric, see 8064;
       For Waterways, see 8500

7950.1 Statistics

7950.2 Congresses

7950.3 Legislation

7950.4 Administration

7955   Economic considerations

7980   Flow control. Flood control

7980.3 Watersheds

7980.5 Flood plain

7980.7 Finances

7990   Supply and distribution

7991   Rural water supply

7992   Use in industry

7995   Surface water

7996   Water underground (ground water)

8000   Sanitary treatment

8010   Pollution and pollution control. Thermal
       pollution and control

8020   Sewerage

8022   Sewage treatment

8025   Insect control and pesticides

8040   POWER AND ENERGY

8060   Production and distribution

8061   Statistics

8062   Distribution

8063   Electric

8064   Hydroelectric

8066   Fuels

8066.1   Mineral. Coal

8066.2   Petroleum

8066.3   Natural gas

8067   Nuclear energy
8068   Solar energy
8069   Use
8075   Rural distribution
8084   Other

       INDUSTRY, TRADE, SERVICES, MANAGEMENT
8100   General
8100.1   Specific industries
8100.2   Economics of industry
8100.25   Social considerations
8100.3   Taxation
8100.4   Nationalization of industry
8100.5   Statistics
8100.6   Industrial relations
8100.7   Defense industries

8101   LOCATION OF INDUSTRY
8101.1   Technical procedure
8101.2   Diversification
8101.3   Relocation
8101.4   Economics
8101.5   Local promotion
8101.6   Relation to community
8101.7   Relation to planning
8102   Decentralization of industry
8103   Depressed areas
8104   Industrial parks; Industrial estates
         Formerly Trading estates
8105   Building industry
8110   Manufacture
8112   Food and kindred products
8113   Marketing. Wholesale trade
8122   Foreign trade
8124   Public services. Cf. 1541.5
8125   Retail trade
8125.5   Statistics

8130 Consumption
8140 Employment
8140.1   Statistics
8141   Employment legislation
8141.5   Specific problems, e.g., minority problems
8142 Employment in agriculture
8143   Labor conditions and labor supply
8145   After-war employment
8147 Public works

8150 HOUSING
8160 Urban
8165 Rural
8170 Subsistence homesteads, Greenbelt towns
8171 Government aid
8171.5 Housing industry
8172 Land settlement

8200 PUBLIC AND QUASI-PUBLIC BUILDINGS AND GROUNDS

8210 ADMINISTRATIVE

8220 EDUCATIONAL
8222   Colleges
8223   Teachers colleges
8225   Schools
8226   Secondary schools
8227   Elementary schools
8228 Libraries
8229 Museums

8229.3 CULTURAL
8229.4   Art centers
8229.5   Music centers

8230 RELIGIOUS

8240 WELFARE
8240.5   Legislation
8240.6   Administration

8242	HOSPITALS
8242.5	Surveys
8243	Legislation
8244	Mental diseases
8245	Tuberculosis
8247	Clinics
8248	Institutional homes
8250	CORRECTIONAL, POLICE
8252	Prisons
8254	Jails and houses of correction
8256	Juvenile
	TRANSPORTATION AND COMMUNICATION
	Theories. Policies
8300	General
8300.01	History
8300.02	Statistics
8300.05	Future considerations
8300.1	Congresses
8300.2	Administration
8300.3	Agencies, commissions
8300.4	International considerations
8300.5	Relation to planning and environment
8300.55	Effect on community. Social effects
8300.56	Economic considerations. Effect on land values
8300.6	Federal aid
8300.7	Taxation
8300.8	Research
8301	Technical procedure. Mathematical models in transportation. Transportation engineering. Automation
8301.1	Transportation networks. Circulation diagrams
8301.2	Transportation systems. Modes (more than one)
8302	Technology
8304	Transportation industry
8304.5	Government ownership

8305	Private ownership
8306	War-time; Military considerations, War-time use
8330	HIGHWAYS
8330.1	Congresses
8330.5	Design and planning
8330.55	Statistics
8330.6	Economic considerations
8330.8	Research
8331	Legislation
8331.1	Acquisition of land
8331.2	Right of way
8332	Administration
8332.5	Surveys
8333	Financial considerations. Federal programs
8334	Toll roads . Toll booths
8335	Highways, Rural
8335.5	Sidewalks, Highways
8336	Construction and maintenance
8337	In cities. Cf. 2175
8337.5	Circumferential
8338	International
8339	Multiple use
8340	Esthetic considerations
8341	Automobile junkyards
8360	Freeways
8360.1	Economic considerations
8360.2	Access
8360.5	Rapid transit use
8370	Parkways
8380	Tourways
8400	Roadside improvement
8401	Legislation
8402	Planting
8403	Public utilities

8410 Highway safety
8415   Grade crossings
8416   Interchanges
8420 Traffic
8422   Regulation. Automated control
8430 Highway common carriers
8432   Passenger (bus)
8432.1   Statistics
8432.2   Economic considerations
8432.3   Terminals
8434   Freight (truck)
8434.1   Statistics
8434.2   Economic considerations
8434.3   Terminals

8450 RAILROADS
8451 Economic considerations
8451.5   Taxation
8452 Statistics
8470 Passenger
8471   Statistics
8472   Economic considerations
8475   Terminals
8480 Freight
8482   Statistics
8483   Economic considerations
8485   Terminals

8500 WATERWAYS
8505 Legislation
8510 Inland. Canals
8515   Ports
8520 Ocean
8525   Ports
8530 Lighthouses

8540   AIRWAYS
8540.2 Surveys
8540.5 Statistics
8540.6 Standards
8541   Congresses
8541.2 Societies
8543   Legislation
8544   Administration
8545   Airports, see also 2795
8545.5   Location
8546   Economic considerations
8548   Helicopter

8560   PIPE LINES
8565   Gas
8570   Oil

8580   COMMUNICATION AND COMMUNICATION LINES
8585   Telecommunication, radio, television

DEMOGRAPHY
8600 General
8601   Population: analysis and estimates
8602   Statistics and vital statistics
8603   Relation to environment
8604   Growth and change
8605   Mobility and movement
8606   Migration
8607   Relocation
8608   Projections and forecasts
8609   Population planning. Birth control

APPENDIX A

Geographic Table

SOURCE

This geographic table is Table II from Library of Congress,
Classification: Class N, Fine Arts, 4th ed., 1970.

LIBRARY OF CONGRESS

Geographic Table

America	01
Latin America	02
North America	03
United States	05
Colonial period; 18th (and early 19th) century	06
19th century	07
20th century	08
New England	10
Middle Atlantic States	.5
South	11
Central	14
West	17
Pacific States	19
States, A-W	25
Cities, A-Z	27
Canada	29
Mexico	31
Central America	33
British Honduras	35
Costa Rica	37
Guatemala	39
Honduras	41
Nicaragua	43
Panama	45
Salvador	46
West Indies	47
Bahamas	49
Cuba	51
Haiti	53
Jamaica	55
Puerto Rico	57
Other, A-Z	58
South America	59
Argentine Republic	61
Bolivia	63
Brazil	65
Chile	67
Colombia	69
Ecuador	71
Guyana (British Guiana)	73
Surinam (Dutch Guiana)	.2
French Guiana	.4
Paraguay	75

```
    Peru                                      77
    Uruguay                                   79
    Venezuela                                 81
Europe                                        83
  Great Britain. England                      85
    England - Local                           87
    Scotland                                  89
    Ireland                                   91
    Wales                                     93
  Austria                                     95
  France                                      97
  Germany                                     99
    Germany (Democratic Republic,
       1949-    )                             100.6
  Greece                                      101
  Italy                                       103
  Netherlands                                 105
    Holland                                   107
    Belgium.  Flanders                        109
  Russia in Europe                            111
      For Caucasian republics,
        see Russia in Asia
  Scandinavia                                 113
    Denmark                                   115
    Iceland                                   117
    Norway                                    119
    Sweden                                    121
  Spain.  Spain and Portugal                  123
    Portugal                                  125
  Switzerland                                 127
  Turkey                                      129
  Other Balkan states                         131
    Bulgaria                                  133
    Montenegro, see 71, 141,
       212, 235 (.Y8)                        (135)
    Rumania                                   137
    Serbia, see 71, 141,
       212, 235 (.Y8)                        (139)
  Other countries, A-Z                        141
    .C9   Czechoslovak Republic
    .F5   Finland
    .P6   Poland
    .Y8   Yugoslavia
Asia.  The Orient[1]                          143
```

---

[1] Use only the indicated number and only for general works on the area as a whole.

```
Southwestern Asia.  Near
    East.  Levant.  Asia
    Minor[1]                          145
  By country, A-Z                     146
    I7   Iraq
    .J6  Jordan
    .L4  Lebanon
    .S2  Saudi Arabia
    .S9  Syria
    .Y4  Yemen
  Israel.  Palestine                  146.6
Iran.  Persia                         147
Central Asia[1]                       149
  Afghanistan                            .6
  Russia in Asia[2]
    By republic, A-Z                  150
    .A7  Armenia
    .A9  Azerbaijan
    .G4  Georgia
    .K3  Kazakhstan
    .K5  Kirghizistan
    .T3  Tajikistan
    .T8  Turkmenistan
    .U9  Uzbekistan
Southern Asia[1]                      150.6
  India                               151
  Ceylon                              152.6
  Pakistan                            153
  Other countries, A-Z                   .6
Southeastern Asia[1]                  154
  Burma                                  .6
  French Indo-China[1]                155
    By country, A-Z                   156
    .C3  Cambodia   (Khmer)
    .L3  Laos
    .V5  Vietnam
  Thailand.  Siam                     156.6
```

-----

[1] Use only the indicated number and only for general works on the area as a whole.

[2] For Russia in Asia as a whole, use the numbers provided for Central Asia.

```
    Malaysia.  Malaya[2]              157
    Indonesia.  Dutch East
        Indies[3]                     159
    Philippine Islands               161
  Eastern Asia[1]                    163
    China[4]                         165
    Japan                            167
    Korea                            168.6
  Other countries, A-Z              172
Africa[1]                           173
  North Africa[1]                   174
    Algeria                            .6
    Libya                              .65
    Morocco                            .7
    Sudan                              .75
    Tunisia                            .8
    Egypt                          175
    Other North Africa, A-Z        176.6
      .I3  Ifni
      .S6  Spanish Sahara
    Ethiopia                           .7
  Eastern Africa[1]                 176.8
    By country, A-Z                    .9
      .B8  Burundi
      .C6  Comoro Islands
      .F7  French Somaliland
      .K4  Kenya
      .M3  Madagascar
      .M6  Mozambique
      .R8  Rwanda
      .S6  Somali Republic
      .T3  Tanzania
      .Z3  Zanzibar
```

---

[1]
    Use only the indicated number and only for general works on the area as a whole.

[2]
    Sabah, Singapore and Sarawak and Malaya are treated as locals of Malaysia here.

[3]
    Java, Sumatra, Kalimantan and West Irian are treated as locals of Indonesia here.

[4]
    Formosa (Taiwan) is treated as a local of China in this table.

Western Africa[1]   177
  By country, A-Z   .6
    .A5 Angola
    .C3 Cameroon
    .C4 Central African Republic
    .C5 Chad
    .C6 Congo (Democratic Republic)
    .C7 Congo (Brazzaville)
    .D3 Dahomey
    .G3 Gambia
    .G5 Ghana
    .G8 Guinea
    .I8 Ivory Coast
    .L5 Liberia
    .M3 Mali
    .M4 Mauritania
    .N4 Niger
    .N5 Nigeria
    .P6 Portuguese Guinea
    .R5 Rio Muni
    .S4 Senegal
    .S5 Sierra Leone
    .S6 Southwest Africa
    .T6 Togo
    .U6 Upper Volta
Southern Africa[1]   178
  By country, A-Z   .6
    .B6 Botswana
    .L4 Lesotho
    .M3 Malawi
    .R5 Rhodesia, Southern
    .S6 Republic of South Africa
    .S8 Swaziland
    .Z3 Zambia
Australia   179
  Special (including
    Tasmania), A-Z   180
New Zealand   181
Pacific islands   183
  Special, A-Z   184
    Hawaiian Islands, <u>see</u>
      10, etc.

_____

[1] Use only the indicated number and only for general works on the area as a whole.

Abstracts, 14.5
Acre, Number of houses to, 1677
ACTION, 518
Addresses, lectures, 265, 542
"Adickes, Lex", 728
Administration quarters (Water-
fronts), 2690
Administrative agents, 1520
  Creation or empowering, 711
Administrative and legal conditions,
1500
Administrative buildings, 3565, 3720,
8210
Administrative conditions, 1520,
  collection and presentation of data,
824
Administrative districts, 1625
Advertising, 540
Advertising kiosks, 3878
Advocate planning, 550
Aerial surveys, see Surveys, aerial,
838
Aerial transportation terminals,
2795
Aerial views, 1244; Maps, 838
Aged, 1212
  Economic needs, 1228
  Housing for, 1430.9
  Recreation for, 1495.9
Agricultural belts, 1720
Agricultural colonies, 5360
Agricultural districts, 1715
Agricultural occupancy of blocks,
3244
Agriculture, 7400
Air, 1447
Air force bases, 5312
Air pollution, 1447
Airports, 2795, 8545
Air raid shelters, 3811
Airways, 2795, 8540
Alarm systems, 2926
Albums (General), 286
Alleys, 2242, (In blocks), 3181
Allotment gardens, 1724
Amusement areas, 4290, 7706
Anchorages (Harbors), 2605
Ancient cities, 215
Animal husbandry, 7440
Annexation, 1520.1
Announcements and brochures, 805
Apartments, 3179, 3641; Districts
  with, 1702

Apportionment, Estimate, 1595
Appraisal of land, 1566.2
Approaches:
  City, 1748
  Elevated or subway stations, 2405
  Highway bridges and tunnels, 2276
  Subways, 2356
Aqueducts (Conduits), 2885
Aqueducts, Monumental, 3740
Arcades, 2161
Archaeologic areas, 4224, 4230, 7750
Arches, Monumental, 3830
Architectural control, 772, 774
Architectural details, 3509
Architectural squares, 4435, 4575
Architectural style, 3490
  Types of city plans distinguished
  by, 5690
Architecture, Civic, see Public
  buildings; Types of city plans
  distinguished by architectural
  style
Arctic regions, 7330.4
Armed Services, 548
Art, Civic, 1235
Art centers, 1629, 8229.4
Art commissions, 1535.1
Artifacts, Prehistoric, 7758
Artificial topography, 1347
Assessment, Income from, 1580
Assessment laws, 722
Asylums, 3585
Athletic fields, 4370, 7695
Atlases, General, 282
Atmospheric sciences, 7159
Atrium houses, 3179, 3636
Audio visual media, 543, 838
Auditoriums, 3575
Authorities, 716, 1525.5
  Transportation, 2025, 2355.1
  Port, 2571
Automation (Data Processing), 817
  Traffic, 2076.3, 8422
  Railroad, 2457
Automation in transportation, 8301
Automobile junkyards, 8341
Automobile service stations, 3685
Automobiles, 2058
Aviation:
  Grounds, 4384
  Influence on planning for appear-
  ance of city, 1246
  Landing places, 2795

INDEX

Backyard gardens, 4902
Balconies (Encroachments on streets), 2159
Balcony gardens, 4914
Ball grounds, 4370, 7696
Bandstands, 3681
Bank deposits, 1429.5
Banks (Buildings), 3600
Banks of rivers, canals, 2590
Barrios, 1704.5
Basins (Water-supply), 4510
Basins, fountains, 3845
Basins, harbors, 2600
Basketball, 4370
Bastides, 5309
Baths, Public, 3580
Bay trees, in tubs, boxes, etc., 4916
Bays, harbors, 2600
Beaches, 7702
Beauty, Civic, 1235
Beer gardens, 4280
Behavioral sciences, 1214
Belt lines (Railroad), 2504
Belts, Agricultural, 1720
Belts, Forest, 1725
Belts of green, 1730, 4158
Benefit assessments, 1580
Bequests, Income from, 1594
Betterment, Civic, see Civic betterment
Betterments, 1580
Bibliography
  General, 0
  See also special subjects
Bicycle paths, 2214
Bicycles, 2076.38
Billboards, 3880
Biography, 200
Bird sanctuaries, 7741
Birdseye views, 1244
Birth control, 1427, 8609
Blackouts, 3814
Blighted (gray) areas, 1613, 1704
Block, Houses in-, see Houses in-block
Blocks (Areas), 3100
  Area, Proportion to street area, 2150
  Development, Adaptability to, 3120
  Dimensions, 3125
  Interiors, 3179
  Orientation, 3140
  Shape, 3130
  Size, 3125
  Topography, 3145
Blocks and lots, 3000
  Development, Adaptability to, 3040
  Dimensions, 3045
  Orientation, 3060
  Redistribution of land, 728, 3040
  Shape, 3050
  Size, 3045
  Topography, 3065
Blocks and streets, Organization

and subdivision of city area into, 1800
Boarding and lodging houses, 3619
Boards of trade, 515
Boating, 4203, 7701
Bomb proof construction, 3545
Bomb resistant construction, 3545, 3810.5
Bombs, Replanning cities destroyed by, 1293
Bond issues, 1578
Books, (General collections), 294
Boom towns, 5629.5
Booths, street-stands, 3684
Botanic interest, 7735
Botanical gardens, 4265
Boulevards, 2207
  Planting, 4893
Boulevards, Shore, 4196
Boundaries
  City, 1745
  Lots, Treatment, 3304
  National, 7080
Boundary areas (Of city), 1745
Boundary structures (Walls, fences), 3825
Breakwaters, 2617
Breweries, 3595
Brick and tile (Buildings materials), 3523
Brick-yards, 3197
Bridges, 3740
  Design, 3770
  Materials, 3780
Bridges, Covered, 3771
Bridges, Foot, 2262
Bridges, Highway, 2270
Bridges, Over rivers, canals, 2595
Bridges, Railroad, 2515
Bridges, Street-railway and transit, 2390
Bridle paths, 2213, 7715
Budgets, 1570.5; For environment, 7150.4
Building and loan associations, 1431.6
Building codes, 3460
Building construction, 3540
Building decoration, 3530
  Vines, etc., 4910
Building groups, 3700
  Grounds, 3440
Building industry, 8105
Building laws, 3460
Building lines, 755, 2157, 3460
Building lots, 3395
Building materials, 3510
  Business districts, 1640
  Types of city plans distinguished by, 5680
Buildings, 3440
  Designs and plans, 3467
  Grounds, 4600
  Height, 3083, 3460, 3480
    Business districts, 1640

Relation to street, 2163
Types of city plans distinguished by, 5630
In parks, 4106
Relation to
  Block and lot area, 3075
  Block area, 3165
  Lot area, 3315
  Streets, 2155
Size, 3480
Surface treatment, 3530
Buildings, Historic, 3456
Bulkhead lines, 2610
Bureaucracy, 1531
Burned districts, Replanning, 1293
Buses, 2350, 2780, 8432
Business and commercial building groups, 3721
Business blocks, 3190
Business buildings, 3600
  Streets as frontage for, 2230
Business districts, 1630
Business encroachment on residential districts, 1678
Business squares, 2233
Business local streets, 2230
Business streets: Planting, 4891
Business traffic streets, 2195

Cables, Underground, 2386
Cabstands, 2199
Campaigns, City planning, 525
Camps, 3573, 4136, 4460, 7670
Campus planning, 3722
Canals, 2580, 3800, 8510
Canals, Irrigation, Streets with, 2118
Cantonments, 5310
Capital improvement programs, 1570.5
Capitols, 3565
Car-barns, 2420
Caves, 7733
Cemeteries, 4480, 7756
Censuses, 830
Centers, Civic, see Civic centers
Central business districts, 1655
Central heating systems, 2902, 3568
Central place, 5324.5
Centers, Determining location of main thoroughfares, 1812
Ceremonies, 2320
Chambers of commerce, 515
Change in type of occupancy, Effects of, 1613
Channels
  Commercial rivers, 2585
  Harbors, 2605
Channels of transportation, 2000
Charts, General, 254
Chemicals, 7900
Chemicals, Areas for handling and storing, 2724
Child care, 3588
Children, 1211
Chimneys, 3504

Circular type of city plan, 5645
Circumferential highways, 2183, 8337.5
Cities:
  Annexation, 1520.1
  Growth, 1416
  Ideal, 5370
  Location, 1340
  New, 5340
  Size, 5600
Cities, Capital, 5305
Cities, History, 1410
Citizen participation, 549
City
  At night. Lighting effects, 1260
  Boundaries, 1750
  Historic forms, 210
  History, 1410
  Organic beauty, 1242
  Sites, 1340
    Economic advantages, 1555
City and country, 1418
City clubs, 517
City-county consolidation, 1524
City engineers' departments, 1530
City forestry, see Vegetation
City gates, 3815
City halls, 3565
City planning
  As an art, science, or profession, 320
  By special countries and cities arranged geographically, 6800
  Definition, 310
  Field, scope, 310
  Goals, 305
  Purpose, utility, 305
  Term, 300
City-planning commissions and departments, 714, 1535
City planning, Enforcing, 750
City planning in literature, 270
City planning movement, 500
City plans:
  Composition, 1200
  Cost, 878
  Elements, 1900
  Historical development, 210
  Location, 1340
  Methods, 815
  Theory, 912
  Types, 5200
City walls, 3815
Cityward movement, 1416
Civic art, 1235
Civic beauty, 1235
Civic betterment (Term), 300
Civic betterment movement, 500
Civic centers, 1627, 3720, 4570
Civic design (Term), 300
Civic improvement, 1235
Civic spaces, see Squares
Civil defense, 3810
Classification, Library, 93
Clay, 1382, 7910
Cliffs, 7727.5

Climate, 1330, 7160
  Climate and planning, 7161
  Types of city plans distinguished
  by, 5210
Climate, Relation to buildings, 3475
Climate, topography, soil, etc., 1320
Climatic aspects of vegetation, 4811
Clinics, 8247
Clippings (General collections), 290
Clocks, 3855
Clubs
  Buildings, 3618
  In City planning movement, 517
Cluster, 3050, 3241
Coal, (storing): 2723; As fuel, 8066.1
Coast cities (Types of plans), 5255
Coasts, 1370
Cold climate, Types of city plans
  distinguished by, 5225
Cold storage goods (storing), 2725
Collected works, 180
  City planning study in, 940
  Collections of material in special
  forms, 280
College housing, 1434.35
Colleges, 3571, 8222
Colleges, Study and teaching of
  city planning in, 935
Collision points, Avoidance, 2136
Colonnaded streets, 2161
Color
  Aspects of city, 1256
  Building materials, 3517
Combustible type of building
  construction, 3544
Comfort stations, 3677
Commerce, Chambers of, 515
Commercial buildings, 3210, 3600
Commercial cities (Types of plans),
  5315
Commercial opportunities, 1559
Commercial structures, 3210, 3721
Commercial and recreational use
  of waterfronts, 4177
Commercial waterways and water-
  fronts, 2550, 8500
Commissions:
  Art, 1535.1
  City planning, 1535
    Creation, 714
Common carriers, 8430
Commons, 4245
Communication, 8580
Community centers, 1627
Community colleges, 3571
Community kitchens, 3615
Community planning (Term), 300
Commuting, 2006
Company towns, 5347
Competitions, 880
Composite type of informal plat,
  1851
  Types of city plans, 5651
Composition of city plan, 1200
Comprehensive plans, 850

Comprehensive treatises, 250
Concert gardens, Open-air, 4280
Concessions, Private, In parks, 4108
Concourses, 2211
Concrete buildings, 3526
Condemnation of land, 722
Conditions, Direct improvement of, 565
Conditions, Fundamental, 1300
Condominiums, 1431.5
Conduits, Wires, 2850
Conferences, 40
Conflagrations, 1479
Congestion of population, 1420.1
Congestion of traffic, 2057
Congregating places, 4430
Congresses, 40
Conservation, 1567.1, 4026, 7143, 7180,
  7320, 7352
Conservation and restoration of
  buildings, 3417, 3457
Consistency, in general effect of
  buildings, 3455
Constitutional law, 700.1
Construction, Types of buildings,
  3540
Construction and maintenance:
  Blocks and lots, 3028
  Buildings, 3468
  Channels of transportation, 2028
  Direction or supervision of, 860
  Housing, 1433
  Parks and reservations, 4128
  Playgrounds, 4338
  Streets, roads. Footways, 2078
  Study and teaching, 918
  Vegetation, 4840
Consultation of experts, 875
Consumption, 7187, 8130
Contracts and specifications, 859
Conventions, City planning, 40
Conveyor belts, 2245
Cooperation of experts, 875
Cooperative movement, see Copartner-
  ship housing; Garden cities
Copartnership housing, 1431.5
Copings, 4846
Corner lots, 3308
Corner reservations, 3183
Correctional institutions, 3568, 8250
Corridor development, 7043
Cost:
  Blocks and lots, 3029
    See also High-cost, Low-cost,
    Medium-cost
  Buildings, 3469
  Channels of transportation, 2029
  Lots, 3269
  Parks and reservations, 4129
  Playgrounds, 4339
  Residences (As distinguishing
  residential districts), 1694
  Streets, roads. Footways, 2079
  Vegetation, 4842
Cost and standard of living, 1428
Cost benefit analysis, 1572

Cottages, 3654
Councils of government, 1521
Country and city, 1418
Country clubs, 4298
Country parks, 4240
Countryward movement, 1417
County planning, 7010
Courthouses, 3565
Courts, 2238
 Blocks, 3179
 Blocks and lots, 3089
 Garden, 4903
Covered street-ways, 2161
Crematories, 4485
Crime, 1213
Cropping, 7410
Crossings, Railroad, 2510
 Grade, 2512
Crossings, Street, 2128
Cul-de-sac, 1844
Cultural centers, 1628
Culverts, 2286
Curbs, 2122
Curvilinear type of informal plat,
 1849
 Types of city plans, 5649
Custom house, 2690
Cybernetics, 818

Dams, 3800
Data, 817
Data banks, 830
Data processing, 817
Day nurseries, 3588
Dead, Disposal of the, 1483, 4480
Decentralization, 1417, 7260, 8102
Decentralization for defense, 3807
Decision making, 819.5
Decoration, Building, Vegetation,
 4910
Decoration and ornament, Building,
 3530
Decoration for street festivals,
 2320
Defacements of waterfronts, 4179
Defense, 1480
Defensive works:
 Harbors, etc., 2625
 Reservations, 7830
 Structures, 3810
Definition of terms, 310
Delinquency, 1213
Demography, 1405, 8600
Density of development, 1567.4,
 3075, 7342
 Business districts, 1640
 Residential districts, 1677
Departments, City, 1530
 City planning, 1535
 Creation, 714
Depressed areas, 1613, 1704, 8103
Deserted towns, 5629
Deserts, 7330.3
Design:
 Blocks and lots, 3027

Building groups, 3710
Buildings, 3467
Channels of transportation, 2027
General theory and principles, 1200
Parks and reservations, 4127
Playgrounds, 4337
Streets, roads. Footways, 2080
Study and teaching, 914
Design, Planting, 4835
Detached houses, see Houses, Detached
Diagonal and gridiron type of plat,
 1839
 Types of city plans, 5639
Diagonal thoroughfares, 2184
Diagrams (General), 254
Dictionaries, 190
Dikes, 3800
Directories, 195
Disposal of wastes, 1460
Districts, 1600
 Administrative, 1625
 Agricultural, 1715, 7400
 Burned, Replanning, 1617
 Business and commercial, 1630
 Financial, 1667
 Industrial, 1650, 8101
 Manufacturing, 1650, 8110
 Market, 1660
 New, 1610
 Residential, 1675
 Retail, 1670
 Shipping, 1657
 Warehouse, 1657
 Wholesale, 1665
Docking apparatus, 2670
Docks, 2660
Documentation, 817
Domes, 3502
Doors, 3506
Dooryard gardens, 4901
Dormitories, 1434.35
Double-deck streets, 2119
Drain inlets, 2124
Drainage of land, 1452, 4844, 7550
Drainage systems:
 Subsurface, 2895
 Surface, 2890
Drawings
 General collections, 284
Draws:
 Highway bridges, 2278
 Railroad bridges, 2524
Dredging, 2605
Drill grounds, 4395
Drinking fountains, 3849
Drinking troughs, 3849
Drives, 2205
 Shore, 4196
Drydocks, 2735
Dumps, 1472
 Municipal, 4538
Dust prevention, 1450

Earthquakes, 1392
 Replanning cities destroyed by, 1293

INDEX

Earth sciences, 7170
Earthwork, 1347
Easements, Creation of, 735
Ecology, 1320, 1567.2, 4011.1, 7174, 7351
Ecology, Human, 1214, 7150
Economic and financial conditions, 1545, 7200
Economic aspects:
 General, 1225
Economic geography, 1322, 7173
Ecosystem, 7140
Education, Public, 1490
Education of public in city planning, 540
Educational building groups, 3722
Educational buildings, 3570, 8220
Educational cities (Types of plans), 5325
Educational districts, 1628
Efficiency of the community, 1225
Ekistics, 1416
 Study and teaching, 912
Electric power, 8063
Electric services, 2915
Electrification of railroads, 2457
Electroliers, 3870
Elements of city plans, 1900
 Study and teaching, 916
Elevated transit, 2390
Embankments, Shore, 4197
Eminent domain, 722
Employees:
 Accommodation for (Commercial waterfronts), 2690
 Recreation for, 3199
Employment, 1438, 8140
Enabling legislation, 711
Encroachments:
 Buildings on street, 2159
 Business in residential districts, 1678
 Forests, 7622
 National parks, 7688
 Parks, 4106
Encyclopaedias, 190
Energy, Power and, 8040
Enterprises, Municipal, Income from, 1588
Entrances, City, 1748
Environment, 1320, 1400, 4026, 4850, 7140, 7350, 8300.5, 8603
Environmental agencies, 713, 1530
Environmental control, 759
Environmental design, 7143.5
Equal rights, 1516
Equipment, Municipal, Areas for storage, 4540
Erosion, 7560
Erosion, Water, 7565
Erosion, Wind, 7570
Essays (General), 265
Estates, Large private, 3385
Esthetic aspects:
 General, 1235

Legislation, 772
Estimate and apportionment, 1595
Estimates, 858
Estuaries, 1370
Evacuation camps, 5314
Evolution of cities, 1416
Excerpts (General collections), 290
Excess condemnation, 724
 Income from, 1583
Exhibitions, City planning, 50
 In city planning movement, 546
 Study of city planning in, 940
Expenditure, Municipal finance, 1595
Experts:
 Consultation, cooperation, 875
 Public consultation, 1540
 Unofficial employment, 571
Exposition building groups, 3724
Exposition grounds, 4585
Express ways, See Freeways
Extensions, 1610

Factories, 3595
Fair grounds, 4295, 7707
Family, 1211
Farming, 7400
Federal agencies, 1521
Federal aid, 1590
Federal buildings, 3560
Federal grants, 1590
Fences, 3304, 3825
Ferries, 2675
Ferry slips, 2675
Fertilizers, 7900
Festivals, Street decoration for, 2320
Fiction, 270
Filling of low or submerged areas, 1347
Films, 543
Filtration plants, Water-supply, 4510
Financial conditions, 1570, 7282
Financial districts, 1667
Fire, Replanning cities destroyed by, 1293
Fire alarm boxes, 2296
Fire insurance, 3541
Fire prevention, 1478
Fire-proofing, 3543
Fire protection, 1478
 Waterfronts, 2652
Fire-protection water-supply, 2888
Fire-resistive construction, 3542
Fire stations, 3568
Fires, 1479; Forest, 7604
Fish hatcheries, 7749
Fish preserves, 7748
Fishing, 7746
Flagpoles, flagstaffs, 3857
Floating cities, 5260
Flood, Replanning cities destroyed by, 1293
Flood control, 1454, 3800, 7980
Flower beds, Street planting, 4887

Food and kindred products, 8112
Footbridges, 2262
Footways, 2250
Forum, 4430
Forecasts, 831, 7156
Forest belts, 1725
Forest reservations, 4160
Foresters, 4161, 7602
Forests, Municipal, Income from, 1588
Forests and forestry, 7600
Formal types of plats, 1835
  Types of city plans, 5635
Fortifications, Forts, 3812, 7751
Foundation planting, 4911
Foundations (institutions), 521
Fountains, 3845
Franchises, Income from, 1585
Free ports, 2829
Freeways, 8360
Freight, Special provision for
  waterfronts, 2710
Freight houses and yards, Railroad, 2495
Freight terminals, 2820
Freight transportation, see
  Transportation, Freight
Freight tunnels, Railroad, 2522
Frontage:
  Business buildings, 2230
  Lots, 3310
  Waterfronts, 2650
Fuels, 7880, 8066
Fundamental conditions, 1300
Funicular railroads, 2430
Furniture, Park, 4141
Furniture, Street, 2290
Furniture, Street and park, 3860
Future planning, 1290

Galleries, Street, 2161
Game farms and preserves, 7744
Game theory, 837
Games, see Sports and games
Garages, 3509.2, 3608, 3672
Garages, Municipal, 4540
Garages, Parking, 2059.21, 2059.4
Garages, Private, 3672
Garbage disposal, 1472, 4540
Garden apartments, 3179, 3641
Garden cities, 5350
Garden city movement, 582
Garden squares, 4245
Garden suburbs, 1685
  Types of plans, 5350
Garden villages (Types of plans), 5350
Gardens, 3089, 3329, 4900
  Allotment, 1724
  Backyard, 4902
  Balcony, 4914
  Botanical, 4265
  Concert and beer, 4289
  Courtyard, 4903
  Dooryard, 4901

Historic, 7754
  Penthouse, 4919
  Public, 4940
    Planting, 4940
  Rock, 4909
  Roof, 4919
  School, 4907
  Vacant lot, 4905
  Vegetable, 4909
  Window, 4914
Gas distribution systems (Conduits, etc.), 2900, 8565
Gas-leaks, Underground (Injury to vegetation), 4858
Gas tanks, 3568
Gates, 3825
Gates, City, 3815
General collections of material in special forms, 280
General works, 250
Geodesic domes, 3548
Geographic considerations, 1321
Geographical arrangement of special countries and cities, 6800
Geography, 7172
Geological character of soil, 1382
Geology, 7171, 7730
Geysers, 1392
Ghetto, see Racial problems
Ghost towns, 5629
Gifts, Income from, 1594
Glossaries, 190
Golf courses, 4385, 7698
Gorges, 7725
Government, Municipal, 1225, 1520
Government documents, 700
Governmental aid, 1590, 8171
Governmental cities (Types of plans), 5305
Grade separation, 2138
Grade crossings, 2512, 8415
Gradient of streets, 2100
  Steep, 2103
Grain elevators, 2722
Graphic arts, 284
Graphic media, 543
Grass, see Turf
Grasslands, 7330.2
Gravel, 7910
  Areas for handling and storing
    (Waterfronts), 2723
  Soil, 1382
Gravel pits, 1653, 7911
Grazing, 7450
Green belts, 1730, 4158, 4937
Greenbelt towns, 8170
Greenhouses, 3687
  Municipal, 4545
Greens, 4245
Gridiron and diagonal type of plat, 1837, 1839
  Types of city plans, 5637, 5639
Ground forms, see Topography
Ground water, 1380
Grounds:

Building groups, 4550
Single buildings, 4600
Station, 2485
Growth and evolution of cities, 1416
Gutters, 2122
Gymnasia, 3580

Handicapped, 1212.5
Housing for, 1430.9
Transportation facilities, 2760
Villages for, 5355
Hangars, 2795
Harbor boards, 1530
Harbor lines, 2610
Harbors, 2600
Health, Public, see Public health
Health and safety:
General, 1215
Health centers, 3580
Health resorts (Types of plans),
5333
Heating plants, 3568
Heating systems, Central, 2902
Hedges (Lot boundary), 3304
Height of buildings, see Buildings,
Height
Helicopters, 2795, 8548
Herbaceous plants, 4862
High-cost multiple houses in-block,
3642
High-cost residences, 3631
High-cost residential districts,
1695
High-cost single detached houses,
3652
High-cost single houses in-block,
3637
High-rise apartments, 3642.1
High-rise building, 3489, 5660
Highway bridges, 2270
Highway common carriers, 8430
Highways, 2170, 8330
Highways, Interurban, 2170
Hiking, 7712
Hills, (Topographical data), 1356
Removal, 1347
Hills and mountains, 4220, 7727
Hillside cities, 5285
Hillside lots, 3295
Hillside streets, 2103
Hilltop cities (Types of plans),
5290
Historic aspects:
General, 1270
Historic city plans, 1272
Historic features in cities, 1276
Historic interest, Places of, 4224,
4230, 7750
History of planning, 210
History of the city, 1410
Holiday villages, 7676
Holographs, 838
Home ownership, 1434
Homes, Institutional, see Institutional
homes, 5334, 8248

Homesteads, Subsistence, 8170
Hospitals, 3585, 8242
Hot climate, Types of city plans, 5220
Hotels, 2705, 2795.45, 3618
House lots, 3395
House moving, 1616
Houseboats, 2630
Household activity, 1430.41
Houses, Detached, 3650
Blocks occupied by, 3240
Districts with, 1705
Houses, Historic, 7754
Houses, Number to acre, 1677
Houses in-block, 3635
Blocks occupied by, 3235
Districts with, 1700
Housing, 1430, 8150
Housing, Legislation, 1432
Housing, Industrialized, Pre-
fabricated, 1433.3
Housing, Rural, 1432.8, 1434.7,
8165
Housing codes, 1432.3
Housing industry, 8171.5
Hunting, 7742
Hydrants, 2304
Hydroelectric power, 8064; see also
Water power, 1557

Ideal cities, 5370
Illuminated signs, 3875
Illustrations, 284
Improvement, Civic, Rural, etc.,
see Civic improvement, Rural
improvement, etc.
Improvement of conditions, (City
planning movement), 565
Improvements, Effect on land values,
1566.1
Incinerators, 1472
Income, 1429
Income (Municipal finance), 1575
Indexes, 14.5
Indian relics, 7758
Indian reservations, 7820
Individuality of cities, 1274
Industrial cities (Types of plans),
5320
Park systems for, 4085
Industrial conditions, 1435
Industrial districts, 1630, 8101
Industrial estates, 8104
Industrial housing, 1697
Industrial opportunities, 1559
Industrial parks, 8104
Industrial relations, 8100.6
Industrial structures, 3197.5
Industrial waterfronts, 2740
Industrialized building, 3547
Industrialized housing, 1433.3
Industries, Defense, 5321.4, 8100.7
Industry, 8100; Location, 8101,
Nationalization, 8100.4
Informal types of plats, 1845
Information centers, 3684

INDEX

Information storage and retrieval, 817
Infrastructure, 1305, 7033
Inland ports, 8515
Inland waterways, 8510
Input-output analysis, 7280.7
Insect control, 1452, 4852, 8025
Institutes to promote learning, 979
Institutional homes, 5334, 8248
Institutions for correction, see Correctional institutions, 3568, 8250
Insurance, 3541
Interchanges, 2138, 8416
Intergovernmental relations, 1521
International considerations of conservation, 7185; of environment, 7144; of transportation, 8300.4
International highways, 8338
International parks, 7694
International relations, 7091
Intersection of lines of traffic, 2136
Interstate compacts, 7030.2
Interurban highways, 2170
Interurban transit, 2350
Terminals, 2780
Iron and steel buildings, 3528
Ironwork, 3530
Irrigation, 4844, 7540
Irrigation canals, Streets with, 2118
Island cities (Types of plans), 5260
Island reservations, 4184
Islands, 1372
Isles of safety, 2128

Jails, 3568, 8254
Jetties (Protective works), 2617
Jetties, wharves, piers, etc., 2680
Junctions, Street, 2135
Juvenile leagues, 517
Juvenile institutions for correction, 8256

Kiosks, 3878
Kitchens, Community, 3615

Labor, 1438, 8143
Labor camps, 1434.8
Lake shore reservations, 4182
Lakes, 1370, 1373, 7722
Lamp-posts, 3870
Land acquisition for housing, 1431.2
Land classification, 1564, 7325
Land ownership, 1566.8, 7343
Land reclamation, 1347, 1368, 7500
Land settlement, 8172
Land subdivision, 1800, 3000, 3380
Land tenure, 1566.8, 7343
Land use, 1563, 7320; Urban, 1563
Land values, 1566.1, 7341
Landfill, Sanitary, 1472.5
Landing stages, 2697
Landlord-tenant relations, 1434.6

Landscape, Natural, Preservation, 4021
Landscape improvement, 584
Landslides, Replanning cities destroyed by, 1293
Lawns, 4909
Laws, see Legislation
Lectures (General), 265
In city planning movement, 542
Legal and administrative conditions, 1500
Legal conditions, 1505
Legislation, 700
Leisure, 1497
Levees, 3800
"Lex Adickes," 728
Libraries:
Buildings, 3572, 8228
Planning, 90
Study of city planning in, 940
Library science, 91
Lighthouses, 2608, 8530
Lighting, 1476
Lighting, Park, 4143
Lighting, Playground, 4343
Lighting effects, 1260
Lighting fixtures, 3870
Linear programming, 837
Linear type of city, 5635
Lines, Building, 2157, 3081
Loam, 1382
Locks, Canal, 2588
Lodging and boarding houses, 3619
Lot boundaries, Treatment, 3304
Lot planting, 4900
Lots, 3250
Depth, 3311
Development, 3270
Dimensions, 3275
Grade, 3312
Orientation, 3290
Shape, 3280
Size, 3275
Subdivision of blocks into, 3160
Topography, 3293
Low areas, Filling of, 1347
Low-cost multiple houses in-block, 3644
Low-cost residences, 3633
Low-cost residential districts, 1697
Low-cost semi-detached houses, 3659
Low-cost single detached houses, 3654
Low-cost single houses in-block, 3639
Lumber, Areas for handling and storing (Waterfronts), 2723
Lumber-yards, 3197

Mailboxes, 2296
Maintenance, see Construction and maintenance
Malls, 2258
Management, 8100
Manhole covers, 2124
Manpower, 1438
Manuals, Library, 92; Writer's, 190
Manufacturing, Buildings for, 3595

Manufacturing cities (Types of plans), 5321
Manufacturing districts, 1650, 8110
Manufacturing plants, 3195
  Utilization of waterfront by, 2740
Manuscripts (General collections), 292
Maps, 834
Marginal uses of land, 7460
Marinas, 2630, 4203, 7701
Marine parks, 4181
Marine structures, 2559
Market districts, 1660
Market gardens, 1723
Market places, 2234, 4425
Market squares, 2234, 4425
Marketing, 8113
Markets, 1443, 2827
  Buildings, 3610
  Relation to terminal facilities, 2827
Marquees, 2159
Marshes, 1352, 7723
Marshes, Cities on, 5255
Masonry, 3524
Mass transportation, 2350
Master plans, 850
Materials, Building, 3510
  Types of city plans distinguished by, 5680
Mechanical equipment, 1433.06, 3550
Medieval cities, 225
Medium-cost multiple houses in-block, 3643
Medium-cost residences, 3632
Medium-cost residential districts, 1696
Medium-cost semi-detached houses, 3658
Medium-cost single detached houses, 3653
Medium-cost single houses in-block, 3638
Megalopolis, 1504, 5627
Memorial areas and parks, 4025
Men in city planning movement, 587
Mental diseases, Hospitals for, 8244
Metals, 7890
Methodology, 815
Methods of technical procedure
  Professional practice, 800
Metropolitan districts, 1503, 1524
Microclimate, 1331
Migration, 8606
Migratory settlements, 5314.2
Military cities and installations, 5311
Military considerations, 1480
Milk supply, 1443
Mills, 3595
Mineral resources, 1557, 1652, 7732, 7920, 8066.1
Mines, 1652, 7850
Mining, Strip, 7575
Mining cities (Types of plans), 5322
Minor buildings, 3670
Minor streets, Location, 1820
Minor structures, 3820, 3890
Minority problems, 1210.8, 1434.4, 1619, 8141.5
Mission towns, 5375
Mobile homes, 1434.9; Subdivision, 3095
Model cities, 1613.5
Model laws, 712
Model tenement legislation, 1432.37
Models, 836
Models, Mathematical, 833, 8301
Modern cities, 230
Modes, Transportation, 2000, 8301.2
Monorails, 2350
Monumental arches, 3830
Monumental squares, 4435, 4575
Monumental statues, 3840
Monumental waterfronts, 3739
Monuments, 3830; National, 7750
Moorings, 2605
Motels, 2705, 2795.45, 3618
Motor traffic, Influence on streets, 2058
Motor trucks, see Trucks
Mountain villages, 5285
Mountains, 7727
Moving buildings, 1616
Multiple houses in-block, 3641
Multiple streets, 2115
Municipal affairs, 1520
Municipal art, 1235
Municipal buildings, 3563
Municipal finance, 1570
Municipal government, 1225, 1520
Municipal improvement (Term), 300
Municipal improvement movement, 500
Municipal law, 757
Municipal parks, 4100
Municipal services:
  Buildings for, 3568
  Open spaces devoted to operation of, 4500
Museums, 70
  Buildings, 3570, 8229
  In parks, 4106
Music centers, 1629.1, 8229.5
Music shells, 4280

Name (City planning), 300
Nameplates, Street, 2292
Names, Street, 2056
National monuments, 7750
National planning, 7070
Natural features, 4224, 4225
Natural formations, 7733
Natural gas, 8066.3
Natural resources, 1557, 7180.2, 7320
Naval cities and installations, 5313
Neighborhood centers, 1627, 3578
Neighborhood conservation, 1613.1
Neighborhood parks, 4245
Neighborhood units, 1676
Networks, Transportation, 2000
Night, Lighting effect in city, 1260
Noise prevention, 1451
Notes (General collections), 292
Nuclear blasts, 1479, 3810.5

Resistant construction, 3545, 3810.5
Nuclear energy, 8067
Nuclear power, Structures for, 3546, 3568
Nuclear work, 5321.5
Nuisances, 1448; Billboard, 3880
Nurseries, Day, 3588
Nurseries (Plants), Municipal, 4545

Obelisks, 3830
Obsolescence, Housing, 1433.39
  In cities, 1611
Obstruction of surface traffic by transit, 2357
Obstructions to traffic by open spaces, 4015
Oceanic sciences, 7949
Oceans, 7721
Occupancy:
  Change in type, Effects, 1613
  Intensiveness
    Business, industrial districts, 1640
    Residential districts, 1677
Off road vehicles, 2215
Office buildings, 3600
  Blocks occupied by, 3205
Offices, Experience in, 950
Official agencies in city planning movement, 569
Oil, Areas for handling and storing, Waterfronts, 2724
Oil fields, 7921
Oil lines, 8570
One-way streets, 2201
Open-air concert gardens, 4280
Open space, 1568.5, 2238, 4000, 7355
Open space between buildings, 3089, 3179
Opera houses, 3575
Operations research, 819
Opportunities for city planning as an art, science, or profession, 324
Orchards, 7445
Organic beauty of city, 1242
Organizations in city planning movement, 510. See also Societies, 20
Orientation:
  Blocks, 3140
  Blocks and lots, 3060
  Buildings, 3470
  Lots, 3290
  Streets, 2090
Origin and destination, 2076.1
Ornament, See Decoration and ornament
Outer space, 7097
Outlines (General), 254
Outlooks, 4220, 7728
Overhead wires, Removal of, 2922
Overpasses, 2138

Pageants, Settings for, 4275
Paintings (General collections), 284

Pamphlets (General collections), 294
Parades, 2320
Park departments, 1530
Park furniture, 4141
Park regulation, 4120
Park systems, 4040, 7680
Parking, 2059
Parking garages, see Garages, Parking
Parks, 4100, 7675
Parks, Amusement, 4290
Parks, Country, 4240
Parks, County, 7678
Parks, International, 7694
Parks, National, 7685
Parks, Neighborhood, 4245
Parks, Planting, 4935
Parks, Regional, 7677
Parks, Small, 4245
Parks, State, 7680
Parks, Street-transit, 4290
Parks, Water, see Shore reservations, 4170
Parks, Zoological, 4270
Parks and reservations, 4100
Parkways, 2209, 8370
  Planting, 4893
Parliamentary practice, 190
Passageways, 3091, 3181
Passenger terminals, 2800
Passenger transportation, See Transportation, Passenger
Passengers, Provision for (Waterfronts), 2695
Paths, Bicycle, 2214
Paths, Bridle, 2213, 7715
Patios, 3179, 4903
Pavements, 2120
Pavilions, 3675
Peace Corps, 548
Peat, 1382
Pedestrians, 2076.38, 2128
Periodicals, 1
Peripheral thoroughfares, 2183
Perishable goods, Areas for handling and storing (Waterfronts), 2725
Pesticides, 1452, 4852, 8025
Petroleum, 8066.2
Picnic grounds, 7704
Photographs, 838; General collections, 286
Piers, 2680
Piers, Recreation, 4199
Pipes, 2880, 8560
Place names, 1279
Plains, 1352
  Cities on (Types of plans), 5270
Planned unit development, 3000
Planning, 7000
Planning, programming, budgeting, 857
Plans (General collections), 282
  See also City plans
Planting, 4800
Planting, Roadside, 8400

Planting design, 4835
Planting strips. 2109
Plants, 4800
Plastic, 3530
Plats, Types of, 1830
 Types of city plans distinguished by, 5630
Platting legislation, 770, 1808
Play areas, **4300**, 7695
Playgrounds, athletic fields, etc., 4300, 7695
 Planting, 4945
Playgrounds, Street, 2240
Plazas, see Squares
Pleasure resorts (Types of plans), 5333
Pleasure drives, 2205
Pneumatic tube systems, 2905
Pocket-books (General), 258
Pocket parks, 4245
Poles and wires, 2294, 2386
Police, 1213.5, 8250
Police-boxes, 2296
Police stations, 3568
Political science, 1524.5
Politics and planning, 1524.6
Pollution, Air, 1447
Pollution, Shore, 4179
Pollution, Thermal, 8010
Pollution, Water, 1458, 8010
Pollution and control, 7149
Polo fields, 7715
Pools, Swimming and wading, 4350, 7702
Population, 1400, 7250, 8600
 Types of city plans distinguished by, 5230
Population planning, 1427, 8609
Porches, 3508
Port regulation, 2570
Portable buildings, 3549
Portfolios (General), 284
Ports, 2550, 8515
 Directors, 1530
 Types of plans, 5317
Postcards (General collections), 286
Posters, 3880
Poverty, 1225
Power, 8040
Power-houses, 3568
Power lines, 2294, 2386, 2915
 Injury to environment, 4856
Practice, Professional, see Professional practice
Practioners, Experience under, 950
Prairies, 1352
Precipitation, 1334
Prefabrication, 1433.3, 3547
Prehistoric artifacts, 7758
Preservation of historic features in cities, 1276
Preservation of natural landscape, 4021
Prices, 1428
Primers, 548

Prints (General collections), 286
Prisons, 3568, 8252
Privacy, Right to, 1214.07
Private concessions in parks, 4108
Private gardens in cities, 4900
Private property laws, 1515
Private ways, 2244
Proceedings:
 Congresses, conferences, conventions, 40
 Societies, 20
Profession of city planning, 320
Professional practice, 800
Programming, 837
Propaganda in city planning movement, 544
Promenades, 2258
 Shore, 4197
Property, Private, Laws, 1515
Property, Public, 720
 Income from, 1588
 Laws, 1510
Protection from floods, 1454
Protective works, Harbors, etc., 2615
Psychological aspects, 1214.05
Public baths, 3580
Public buildings, 3563, 3717, 8200
Public buildings, Historic, 7752
Public comfort stations, 3677
Public finance, 1570
Public gardens, see Gardens, Public
Public health, 1215
Public health and safety, 1445, 7275
Public opinion, 575
Public participation, see Citizen participation
Public property, see Property, Public
Public school systems, 1490.1
Public schools, Teaching city planning in, 548
Public service corporations, 1541
Public services, 1541.5, 8124
Public utilities, 1541, 2850, 8403
 Income from municipal operation, 1588
Public welfare, see Welfare
Public works, 1438
Public works, Departments of, 1530
Publications, City planning movement, 544
Publicity, 540
Pumping stations, 3568

Quality of life, 7155
Quarantine quarters, 2690
Quays, wharves, etc., 2680
Quotations, 300

Race tracks, 4380, 7708
Racial problems, 1210.8, 1434.4, 1619, 8141.5
Radial and round-point type of plat, 1841
 Types of city plans, 5641
Radial thoroughfares, 2182

INDEX

Radiation, 7149
Radio, 2935, 8585
Railings (Protection of vegetation),
  4846
Railroad bridges and tunnels, 2515
Railroad centers (Types of plans),
  5316
Railroad stations, 2480, 3605
Railroad tunnels and bridges,
  2515
Railroads, 2450, 8450
  Bridges, 2515
  Crossings, 2510
  Electrification, 2457
  Government ownership, 2458
  High speed, 2484
  Legislation, 2470
  On wharves, piers, 2714
  Planting, 2460, 2486
  Rights-of-way, 2500
  Stations, 2480, 3605
    Grounds, 2485
  Terminals, 2785, 8475, 8485
  Tunnels, 2515
  Yards, 2490, 2495
Railways, Street, see Street-
  railways
Ramps, Foot, 2256; Highway, 2276
Rapid transit, 2350
  Terminals, 2807
Real estate, 1566.5, 1566.6
Reclamation of land, 1347, 1368,
  7500
Reconstruction, After war, 1293, 1295
Recreation, 1495, 1730, 3199, 3245,
  7650; See also Open spaces, 4000
Recreation areas for employees,
  3199
Recreation buildings and centers,
  1730, 3575, 3728, 4318
Recreation piers, 4199
Recreational waterfronts, 4170, 7700
Rectilinear informal plat, 1847
  Types of city plans, 5647
Recycling, 1461
Redistribution of land, 728, 3040
Reforestation, 7605
Refreshment places, 4139
Refugee camps, 5314.1
Regional accounts, 7031
Regional planning, 7030
Regional science, 7032
Registration, Professional, 811
Rehousing, 1433.8
Reinforced concrete, 3527
Religion, 1210.9
Religious institutions, 3590, 7753,
  8230
Religious towns, 5375
Relocation of cities, 1618
Relocation of population, 1425, 8607
Remote sensing, 838
Replanning, 1293
Reprints, 296
Research, 942

Reservations, 4100, 7800
  Corners, 3183
  Separate roadways, 2109
  Street-railway and transit, 2382
Reservations, Indian, 7820
Reservoirs, 4210, 4510
Residences, 3620; see also Houses
Residences, Grounds, 4900
Residential blocks, 3230
Residential cities (Types of plans),
  5330
Residential districts, 1675
Residential lots, 3380
Residential squares, 2238, 4445
Residential streets, 2235
  Planting, 4892
Resorts, Health and pleasure (Types
  of plans), 5333
Resources, Economic and financial,
  1545; Natural, 1557, 7180.2, 7320
Restaurants, Outdoor, 4139
Resting places, (Parks, etc.), 4137
  Roadside, 7728
Restoration, see Conservation and
  restoration
Restrictions
  Appearance of buildings, 3460
  Blocks and lots, 3020
Retail districts, 1670
Retail shops, 3600
Retail trade, 8125
  Blocks occupied by, 3210
Retirement of land, 7465
Revenue service quarters, 2690
Ribbon development, 1671
Riding trails and polo fields,
  7715
Rights-of-way
  Creation, 735
  Highway, 8331.2
  Railroad, 2500
Rights, Laws relating to:
  Equal, 1516
  Private, 1515
  Public, 1510
River bank reservations, 4183
River cities (Types of plans), 5265
Rivers, 1373, 4183, 7724;
  Commercial waterways, 2580
Roads, 2050
Roads, Park, 2212, 4145
Roadside improvement, 4875, 8400
Roadside parks, 7728
Roadside planting, 4875, 8400
Roadside stands, 3684
Roadways, Separate, 2107
Rocks, 1382
Roof gardens, 4919
Roofs, 3504
Round-point and radial type of
  plat, 1841
  (Types of city plans), 5641
Round-points, 2197
Routes, Determining location of
  main thoroughfares, 1814

Rubbish disposal, 1472
Running tracks, 4370
Rural areas, 7370
Rural communities, 5361
Rural housing, 1432.8, 1434.7, 8165
Rural improvement movement, 584
Rural planning, 7370
Rural zoning, 1622

Safety, Isles of, 2128
Sand, 1382, 7910
Sanitariums, see Hospitals
Sanitary landfill, 1472.5
Sanitation, 1445
Satellite towns, 5345
Scale, in buildings, 3455
Scales, City, 3872
Scenic areas, 4231, 7720
School gardens, 4907
School playgrounds, 4319
Schools
  Buildings, 3570, 8220
  For study and teaching of
  city planning, 979
Schools, Public, Teaching city
  planning in, 548
Screen plantations; Highway, 4875;
  Yard, 4900
Sculpture, Municipal, 3840
Seashore reservations, 4181
Seashores, 1370, 7721
Seats, 3860
Sea walls, 2619
Segregation. See Racial problems
Semi-detached houses, 3656
  Districts with, 1707
Series. Collected works, 180
Services, 8100
Services, Municipal, see Municipal
  services
Setbacks, 755, 2157
  Legislation, 2073
Sewage disposal, 1464, 8020
Sewage disposal areas and
  plants, 4520
Sewerage boards, 1530
Sewerage systems, 2890
Sheds, Freight (Wharves), 2718
Shelters, 3675
  Parks, etc., 4137, 7665
  Playgrounds, 4345
  Street-railway and transit, 2410
  Wharves, etc., 2699
Shipbuilding plants, 2744
Shipping districts, 1657
Shipyards, 2735
Shooting grounds, 7743
Shop signs, 3882
Shops, Retail, 3600
  Blocks occupied by, 3210
Shore boulevards, 4196
Shore cities (Types of plans), 5255
Shore reservations, 4170
Shores, 1360
Shrubs, 4861

Street planting, 4886
Sidewalk obstruction, 2159
Sidewalks, 2252, 8335.5
Signs, Commercial
  Illuminated, 3875
  Shop, 3882
Silhouette (of city), 1248
Single detached houses, 3651
  Districts with, 1706
Single houses in-block, 3636
  Districts with, 1701
Site planning, see Land subdivision
Sites, City, 1340
  Advantages, etc., 1555
Skating rinks, 4385
Sketches (General collections), 284
Skiing, 7710
Skylines, 1248
Skyscraper cities (Types of city
  plans), 5660
Skyscrapers, 3489
  Business districts, 1640
Slides, 543
  General collections, 288
Slips, Ferry, 2675
Slopes, 1356
Sloping sites, Cities on
  (Types of plans), 5285
Slums, 1704
Smog, 1447
Smoke (Injury to vegetation), 4854
Smoke prevention, 1449
Snow removal, 1475
Snowmobiles, 2215, 4205, 7709.1
Social centers, Playgrounds as,
  4318
Social conditions, 1210, 1400, 7200
  Surveys and studies, 822
Social ethics, 1210
Social sciences, 1210
Societies, 20, 513
Soil, 1380, 7402
  Geological character, 1382
  Preparation and cultivation
  for planting, 4844
  Surveys, 1382
Soil. Groundwater, 1380
Soil erosion, 7560
Solar energy, 8068
Solid waste, 1470
Space, 1567
Space, Outer, 7097
Space requirements, 1567.3, 7353
Space stations, 7097.1
Special districts, 1525.5
Specifications and contracts, 859
Speedways, 4380
Spires, 3502
Sports and games, 4300, 7695
Spraying, 4852
Squares, 4400
  Architectural, 4435, 4575
  Business, 2233
  Garden, 4245

Market, 2234, 4425
Monumental, 4435, 4575
Residential, 2238, 4445
Station, 2485, 4423
Traffic, 2197, 4420
Squatter communities, 1704.5
Stables, Municipal, 4540
Stadiums, 4375
Stages, Landing, 2697
Standpipes, 3568
State agencies for city planning:
Relation to federal and municipal
agencies, 1527
State buildings, 3563
State documents, 708
State grants (Income for city
planning), 1590
State laws and statutes, 710
State planning, 7050
Station grounds, 2485
Station squares, 2485, 4423
Stations:
Railroad, 2480, 3605
Street-railway and transit, etc.
Non-surface, 2405
Transfer, waiting, 2410
Union, 2483
Statistics, 816
Population, 1407, 8602
Statues, 3840
Steam systems, 2910
Steel and iron buildings, 3528
Steep gradients (Streets, etc.),
2103
Steps, 2256
Stockyards, 3197
Stone
Areas for handling and storing
(Waterfronts), 2723
Buildings, 3524
Stone quarries and gravel pits,
1653, 7911
Stoops (Encroachment on streets),
2159
Storage, Buildings for, 3605
Storage areas, Waterfront, 2730
Storage of municipal equipment,
Areas for, 4540
Stores, 3210
Storm sewers, 2890
Stream pollution, 1458
Streams, 1376
Street-cars, see Rapid transit
Street cleaning, 1474
Street decoration, 2320
Street departments, 1530
Street furniture, 2290
Street intersections, 2135
Street lighting, 1476, 3870
Street nameplates, 2292
Street names, 2056
Street numbering, 2056.5
Street plan in organization and
subdivision of city area, 1800
Influence of traffic on, 2057
Street planting, 2315, 4875

Street-railways and transit, 2350
Street signs, Commercial, 3882
Street stands, 3684
Street systems, 1800
Street traffic, 2076
Street transit bridges and
viaducts, 2390
Street transit parks, 4290
Street transit reservations in
streets, 2382
Street transit structures,
Obstruction of surface traffic,
2357
Streets, 2050
Acquisition by city, 2070
Area, Proportion to block area,
2150
Circulation, 2076.2
Cleaning, 1474
Continuity, 2095
Cross-section, 2105
Decoration for festivals, 2320
Form, 2085
Influence of traffic on, 2057
Furniture, 2290
Gradient, 2100
Junctions, 2135
Length, 2095
Lighting, see Street lighting
Maintenance, 2078
Relation of conduits and wires
to, 2857
Orientation, 2090
Planting, 2315, 4875
Relation of street-railway and
rapid transit lines to, 2356
Relation to
Blocks, 3155
Blocks and lots, 3070
Lots, 3305
Surface, 2120
Traffic control, 2076.3
Width, 2074, 2105
Streets, Colonnaded, 2161
Streets, Double-deck, 2119
Streets, Minor, Location, 1820
Streets, Multi-level, 2119
Streets, Parked, 2116
Streets, Two-level, 2119
Strip mining, 7575
Strips, Planting, 2109
Structures, 3400
Study and teaching of city
planning, 900
Style, Architectural, 3490
General effect of buildings,
3455
Types of city plans distinguished
by, 5690
Subdivision, Land, see Land sub-
division
Submerged areas, Filling, 1347
Subsistence homesteads, 8170
Substructures, 3509.5
Subsurface drainage systems, 2895
Subsurface utilities, 2880

Suburban cities and towns
(Types of plans), 5331
Suburban estates, 3390
Suburban residential streets, 2237
Suburban station grounds, 2487
Suburbs, 1685
Subways, In relation to the street, 2356
Subways, Rapid transit, 2400
Approaches, 2356
Summit reservations, 4220
Sunlight, 1447
Superblocks, 3125
Supervision of construction and maintenance, 860
Surface drainage systems, 2890
Surface street-railways and transit, 2380
Surface water, 1466, 7995
Surveys, Aerial, 838
Surveys, Making, 815
Surveys, Topographical, 820
Swimming pools, 4350
Syllabi (General), 254
Symbols, 835
Systems analysis, 819

Tables (General), 258
Tabulations of data, 830
Tan-yards, 3197
Tax sharing, 1590
Taxation, 7285
Effect on land development, 1566.1
Income from, 1580
Taxi stands, 2199
Teachers colleges, 8223
Teaching of city planning in public schools, 548
Technical procedure, Methods of Professional practice, 800
Technology and science, 1436, 7001, 7147
Technology in transportation, 8302
Telecommunication, 8585
Telephone and telegraph wires, 2930
Television, 2935, 8585
Temperate climate, Types of city city plans distinguished by, 5215
Temperature, 1332
Tenancy, 1434.6
Tenements, 3644
Districts with, 1703
Model law, 1432.37
Tennis courts, 4370, 7697
Terminal facilities, 2750
Terminals
Aerial transportation, 2795
Bus, 2780
Interurban, 2780
Railroad, 2785, 8475, 8485
Transit, 2420
Waterway and waterfront, 2790
Terminus of vistas, 1252
Terms
City planning, etc., 300
Lists of, 190

Terra cotta building materials, 3530
Terraces, 4903
Terracing, 1347
Theatres, 3575
Drive-in, 4275
Open-air, 4275
Thermal pollution and control, 8010
Theses, 295
Thoroughfares, 2170
Location, 1810
Tile and brick buildings, 3523
Toll booths, 2298, 3786, 8334
Toll roads, 8334
Topographical surveys, 820
Topography, 1340, 7172
Blocks, 3145
Blocks and lots, 3065
Lots, 3293
Streets, 2110
Types of city plans distinguished by, 5250
Topology, 1344
Tours, City planning study, 947
Tourways, 2205, 8380
Towers, 3502
Towers, Water, 3568
Town planning (term), 300
Tracks, Street-railway, 2384
Trade, 8100
Trade, Boards of, 515
Trade, Foreign, 8122
Trade, Retail, 8125
Trade, Wholesale, 8113
Trade centers, 5315.2
Trading estate, 8104
Traffic
Open spaces as obstructions to, 4015
Traffic, Highway, 8420
Traffic, Motor, Influence on streets, 2058
Traffic, Surface, Obstruction by street transit structures, 2357
Traffic, in residential districts, 1679
Traffic censuses, Inventory, 2076.1
Traffic regulation, 2075, 2076.3
Traffic squares, 2197, 4420
Trailer camps, 4460
Trailers, 1434.9
Trails, 7712, 7715
Train yards, 2490
Transfer stations, Rapid transit, 2410
Transitional areas, 1568.8, 1753, 7372
Transportation, 2000, 8300
Buildings in connection with, 3605
Relation of business and industrial districts to, 1633
Relation of recreation areas to, 1733
Relation to growth of suburbs,

1687
Influence on streets, 2058
Transportation, Aerial, 2795, 8540
Transportation, Freight, 2379, 2479, 2820, 8434, 8480,
Transportation, Local, Relation of terminal facilities to, 2807
Transportation, Passenger, 2378, 2478, 2800, 8432, 8470
Transshipment, 2829
Treatises, Comprehensive, 250
Tree guards, 4846
Trees, 4860
  Fruit, 4909
  Street planting, 4885
Trees, Roadside and street, 4885, 8402
Tropic regions, 7330.5
Trucks, 2195, 8434
Tubes (Rapid transit, etc.), 2400
Tunnels
  For foot passengers, 2262
  Freight, 2522
  Highway, 2270
  Railroad, 2515
  Rapid transit, 2400
Turf, 4863
Turf strips (Street planting), 4888
Two-level streets, 2119
Types of city plans, 5200

Unbuilt-over area, see Vacant land
Underdeveloped areas, 7035.5
Underground cables, 2386
Underground footways, 2262
Underground gas-leaks (Injury to vegetation), 4858
Underground transit, 2400
Underground water, 1386, 7996
Underpasses, 2138
Underwater communities and cities, 5261
Undeveloped land, Control, 1609
Unemployment, see Employment
Union stations, 2483
United Nations, 7091
U.S. Congressional publications, 703
U.S. Executive Papers, 701
U.S. Judicial Papers, 702
U.S. Laws and Statutes, 707
Universities, 3571, 8222
Universities, Study and teaching of city planning in, 935
University cities (Types of plans), 5325
Urban activity, 1214.06
Urban analysis, 815
Urban coalition, 518
Urban design, 1235
  Legislation, 772
Urban land use, see Land use
Urban planning (Term), 300
Urban renewal, 1613
Utilities, 1541, 2000, 2850, 2915

Utilities, Privately-owned, Acquisition, 740
Utility buildings, 3675, 4137, 4345
Utopias (Types of plans), 5370

Vacant and undeveloped land, 3087, 3177, 3327, 7335
Vacant lot gardens, 4905
Valleys, 1354, 7726
  Cities in (Types of plans), 5280
Vegetable gardens, 4909
Vegetation, 4800
Vertical cities, 5660
Vertical transportation, 2030
  Highway, 2282
  Subway, 2405
  Railroad, 2526
Viaducts, 3740
  Street-railway and transit, 2390
  Streets, 2138
Views, 1250
  Aerial and birdseye, 1244
Village greens, 4245
Village improvement, 5605
Village improvement movement, 580
Villages (Types of plans), 5605
Villages for handicapped, 5355
Vines, 4912
Vistas, 1252
Volcanoes, 1392

Wading pools, 4350
Wages, 1429.4
Waiting stations, 2410, 2699
Walks, 2108, 2252
Walls:
  Lot boundary, 3304, 3825
  Of buildings, 3506
Walls, City, 3815
Walls, Sea, 2619
War, Replanning of cities destroyed by, 1295
Warehouse districts, 1657
Warehouses, 2718, 3200, 3605
Warm springs, 1392
Waste cans, 3860
Waste disposal, 1460, 4540, 7359
Waste lands, 1346
Water, 1360, 1456, 7950
Water, Cities on, 5260
Water, Flow control, 1454, 7980
Water, Ground, 1386
Water, Ornamental, 1265, 3845
Water, Surface, 1466, 7995
Water, Underground, 1386, 7996
Water boards, 1530
Water conservation, 7950
Water erosion, 7565
Water power, 1557; see also Hydro-electric power, 8064
Water resources, 7950
Water sports, 7700
Water supply and distribution, 1456, 2885, 4160, 4510, 7990
  Fire protection systems, 2888
Water table, 1386

INDEX

Water towers, 3568
Water treatment, 8000
Waterfalls, 7724.5
Waterfront lots, 3296
Waterfronts, 1360
Waterfronts, Commercial and
  industrial, 2640, 2550, 2710
Waterfronts, Monumental, 3739
Waterfronts, Recreational, 4170
Watersheds, 4166, 7980.3
Waterways, 8500
Waterways, Inland, 8510
Ways, Private, 2244
Welfare, 1210.10, 7275, 8240
Welfare centers, 3580
Wells, 3849
Wharves, etc., 2680
Wholesale districts, 1665
Wholesale trade, 8113
Wildernesses, 7729
Wildlife, 7740
Wind erosion, 7570
Window boxes and gardens, 4914
Windows, 3506
Winds, 1336
Winter sports, 4205, 7709
Wires, 2850, 2915
Wires, Overhead: Injury to
  vegetation, 4856
Wires and poles, 2294, 2386
Women in city planning movement,
  586
Women's clubs, 517
Wood buildings, 3521
Woodlands, 7330.1, 7600
Workingmens' homes, 1697
Works, Defensive, see Defensive
  works
Works, Protective, see Protective
  works
World centers and cities, 7090
World planning, 7090
Writers' manuals, 190

Yards
  Brick, 3197
  House lot, 4900
  Lumber, 3197
  Municipal, 4540
  Stock, 3197
  Street-railway and transit, 2420
  Tan, (tanning), 3197
  Train, 2490
Yearbooks, 15
Youth, 1211

Zone condemnation, 728
Zoning, 765, 1620; Airport, 2797.6;
  Housing, 1432.3; Land use, 7322.1;
  Parking, 2059.25
Zoological parks, 4270
Zoos, 4270